A
LITTLE
WHITE
LIE

A LITTLE WHITE LIE

Institutional Divisions of Labor and Life

ROBERT E. AGGER

Elsevier · New York

NEW YORK · OXFORD

Elsevier North-Holland, Inc.
52 Vanderbilt Avenue, New York, New York 10017

Distributors outside the United States and Canada:

Thomond Books
(A Division of Elsevier/North-Holland Scientific Publishers, Ltd)
P.O. Box 85
Limerick, Ireland

Library of Congress Cataloging in Publication Data

Agger, Robert E
    A little white lie.

    Includes index.
    1. Social systems. 2. Social institutions. 3. Social values. 4. Division of
    labor. 5. Community. I. Title.
HM131.A33   301.5   78-15884
ISBN 0-444-99052-6

Manufactured in the United States of America

Designed by Loretta Li

TO SIMONA,

a beautiful example of what is humanly possible when institutional partialization fails

Contents

Acknowledgments

It is impossible to acknowledge most of even the predominant influences on the author's development of the thoughts expressed herein, but I would like to mention a few people with whom I had particularly fruitful demystifying experiences during the past few years. These experiences were not entirely unrelated to marvelous dining-sociating-enlightening-political occasions that constituted hallmarks of everyday-life reality across institutions.

A group of us who share the ideas expressed in this book, to varying degrees, met more or less regularly in Toronto and occasionally in Venice. The participants included, in no particular order, Simona Ganassi Agger, Ben Agger, Gad Horowitz, Mirek Disman, Gerry and Valerie Hunnius, and Juanita and Christian Bay. A close friend, Clyde DeBerry, helped me to dissolve the color vision of my earlier life. Ellen Agger helped me to understand more deeply the constrictions and distortions an institutionally divided and hierarchical society has imposed on women generally. She has helped me as well to understand how it is possible to move to open such institutions as medicine or health care while weakening the various dividing lines separating presumably professional from presumably everyday life. Floyd Hunter is a living testament to the narrowness of identifying people as "sociologists."

Manuela Zevi faithfully transcribed my poor English into final manuscript copy. Peter Connelly helped me by his periodically incredulous reactions to the originally much larger and more "way out" manuscript. William Gum proved to me that not all professional book publishing people are of entirely false consciousness, while Edith Lewis, through editing that was incredibly good, helped dramatically in regard to readability and sense of the book. Finally, Dorina Ganassi Storchi helped me to shatter my partialized-person stereotype of mother-in-law while introducing me to the central importance to human beings of good food, good drink, and good companionship—knowledge that has made writing this book and so many other things a set of pleasant multifaceted experiences instead of boring work or ritual sustenance or stereotyped socializing.

ROBERT E. AGGER

Venice, Italy

Introduction

Although almost all the lines of the argument that follows need more extensive treatment, we feel that it is important to open discussion of the main lines as soon as possible. We have a two-part basic thesis. The first part is that the continuing modern emphasis on divisions of labor and life into increasingly specialized, professionalized institutions is increasingly futile. Such developments are increasingly bad for people: they address pseudoproblems, and at the same time they add to real human problems. Such an emphasis, if continued, may result in the demoralization of whole nations and even of all of Western civilization.

The second part of the basic thesis is that it is possible to begin immediately to rebuild human community by arresting and reducing divisions of labor and life. We assert that this can be done in such a way as to even increase the major benefits of our Western scientific/technological civilization.

We contend that in the process of moving toward a new human project, we must give up basic ideas, images, and even words to which we have become very much accustomed. We must relinquish central portions of our basic perspectives, both bourgeois and Marxist, on the world. We must substitute language and perspectives derived from a model of a person, of human nature, that is different from the authoritative model found in both ideological camps. In order to understand this necessity and possibility, we propose to examine the modern divisions of labor and life and the institutions that supposedly are the objective manifestations of these divisions. To support both parts of our thesis, we must reexamine and demystify what are considered self-evident, sacred beliefs of our society.

A
LITTLE
WHITE
LIE

1

The Appearance
of Modernity

Since the coming of industrialization and urbanization, modern societies everywhere have increasingly taken on an appearance distinguished by two kinds of related developments. On the one hand, there is the presence of what we can term "hierarchically partialized individuals." On the other hand, as both backdrop and stage, is what we may call the "institutionally divided society." Although often sensed as more a matter of society's shaping people than the reverse, there is a widespread feeling that people are becoming ever more partialized and the society ever more finely divided. We need not dwell here on the consequences, which for individuals include more alienation, apathy, depression, neurosis, and mental illness as the inward expressions and crime and delinquency as the outward expressions. For society, there are ever greater probabilities of social breakdown, of collapse of the increasingly complex systems. Nearly everywhere there seems to be an

1

increasing incapacity of governments to govern, as larger numbers of their citizens do not obey and as the major institutions and their subsystems run wild and smash into each other or oscillate in patterns increasingly out of control and possibly catastrophic.

If, as we believe, today's problems are very real and very great but the images employed in attempting to understand them are wrong, there is a terrible danger of applying solutions that are totally inappropriate and/or, indeed, of feeling that there are no solutions as one after another effort at problem solving proves futile. Increasingly people are feeling that even problem management or problem coping is just as impossible as problem solving in the maelstrom.

If the images of hierarchically partialized individuals and of the institutionally divided society are wrong or false, we must see what the concepts are that have combined to produce such images. These concepts have become sacred beliefs shared not only by liberals and conservatives but also by most of the left, communists as well as socialists. These concepts must be examined carefully rather than taken for granted, as they are so often today and were in the past.

Let us start with those concepts that center on the nature of human beings, then look at the major beliefs concerning the nature of society. A primary or basic belief is that man has a set of primary or basic needs. These are the economic, the subsistence needs: the famous trio of food, clothing, and shelter. These needs plus the lesser (although often considered higher) needs constitute a kind of hierarchical semianimal, semimachine mosaic of the person, of everyman and everywoman. People are, thus, viewed from the biological-mechanical standpoint as operating as a set of organs/parts that themselves have needs: they have needs for particular inputs, products, services. Remedies or medicines for specific organs or servicing for particular parts are devised for when a person is ill or not functioning well.

Analysis of total persons into parts is the most intelligent way to proceed on such individual problems. Specialization in the production of the things needed for various parts of man is the most efficient, hence most intelligent, way to proceed to keep people healthy or at least functioning. Specialization would extend to such needs as the spiritual and the cultural.

Thus, turning to the society side, people have created specialized institutions that perform both the normal, daily supply tasks and the special remedial or servicing operations. Since human needs to survive, grow and develop, and function efficiently and effectively provide the basis for man's values, we may understand institutions as being human enterprises of a need- and value-related character. These institutions include the economy; the state, nation-state, or government; the society (family, etc.); cultural, including artistic, institutions; education; religion; etc.

These institutional enterprises have two special qualities. First, they are specialized: they concentrate on one or another part or piece of man's ensemble of needs and values. The concentration is evidenced by the adjective describing the institution or subinstitution: "economic," "political," "cultural," "social," etc. Second, they are something greater and more permanent than the persons admitted to membership or office or merely participants therein. They have something of a superhuman quality.

Thus, the partialization of the individual person has its social counterpart in the existence of divided institutions. Hovering around, over, and under individuals and institutions is a sense of scarcity of valuable things, especially a scarcity or ever-present potential scarcity of the basic economic valuables, the fundamental stuff and staff of life. The economic institutions are, thus, the crucial institutions given the nature of people. Efficiency must be understood as the precious human counterpart of, if not improvement upon, animal instincts. And there exists, as a kind of residual, increasingly narrow noninstitutionalized space, so-called everyday life, which itself is being invaded both by partializing institutions and by a sense that economic values are priority even there. It is an everyday life increasingly smothered by a dense set of heavy institutions.

The divisions of labor and life that such an individual/society model has at its core have, unfortunately, seemed to contribute to the generation of the aforementioned problems for both sides of the equation. People appear to have become ever more partialized role players. It would seem that even large doses of tranquilizers cannot begin to meet nearly everyone's condition of fragmentation into

3

diverse, partialized roles so that life seems increasingly a place in which people are lost in intricate labyrinths, Kafkaesque castles.

Lest anyone think that we are speaking only of conditions in advanced capitalist or welfare states, that person would be mistaken. The authorities of such states as the Soviet Union and various Eastern European countries bemoan alcoholism, crime and delinquency, mental breakdowns, and the like, as do their counterparts in the West. But from our point of view, despite the reliance placed, in communist regimes, on planning by central political and economic authorities, these regimes have misread and misunderstood the nature of the modern problems as much as have their liberal and conservative colleagues or rivals in noncommunist states.

We have suggested and we now say flatly that the foregoing ideas about both individuals and society are wrong. Our next task is to examine the major ideas specified so far to see why they are wrong before offering an alternative understanding of the reality of modern life and its possible directions in future.

We shall start with the concept that people have primary needs, biological or animalistic needs for subsistence, for provisioning, for keeping body alive. This concept depends on dividing man into body and mind—the famous body-mind duality. It also depends on a sense that in nature, without human intervention, the valuable things that can satisfy these needs are scarce and also that in nature there are objects categorizable as economic in the sense of provisioning the body. Such a concept, then, involves substituting for a person a biological/physical/chemical entity. Instead of being seen as a person with a unity of body and mind, man is understood as being a complex of organs or parts consisting of brain, head, and the like above the neck and stomach and the like below, with enveloping skin, etc. And instead of nature consisting of "stuff," meaningless to people until people begin to be conscious of it as a potentiality, as potentially valuable for their various wants, somehow nature is filled with preexisting, already symbolized objects that are there as a result of God's or nature's actions and are awaiting people's use or their acts of further transforming them to satisfy their particular, discrete needs.

From early philosophic times, human life was understood as divisible into at least two discrete parts, into nonoverlapping categories of work and leisure pursuits. It is little wonder that the second category became the "higher" while the former became the more basic and, in that necessary although insufficient sense, the more important.[1] Without food, clothing, and shelter, how can people afford to paint, to sculpt, to dance, and to play?

Without trying to trace Western philosophic development here, we do need to emphasize how fundamental in a manifold of ways was this belief in a duality of man. It affected thinking and action in regard to the Cartesian God-World-I partition, it was involved in the currents of idealism and materialism that shaped philosophical as well as political ideological disputes, and it manifested part of both Marxist and many non-Marxist theories. There was an unshakable conviction that the economic values were the supreme, the primary, the fundamental values. They provided the basis, the infrastructure or the basic structure, for the various superstructures erected and drawing sustenance therefrom. Keeping a person alive rather than saving the person's soul became the prime goal, and keeping a person alive meant that first of all the discoveries of anatomy, biology, physiology, and the beginnings of modern science were keeping the person's body vital, the heart pumping, the blood circulating, and the digestive system operating. Then there would be time and possibility for concerns with the higher matters of mind, culture, and spirit. *The* political problem became one of who would control the basic structure, the economy, the economic institutions, and it is still the central or even the only important problem for many people.[2]

Listen to the atomic physicist Werner Heisenberg comment on the body-mind duality and some of its modern effects. Speaking of the period following Descartes, Heisenberg notes:

Philosophy and natural science developed on the basis of the polarity between the "res cogitans" and the "res extensa," and natural science concentrated its interest on the "res extensa." The influence of the Cartesian division on human thought in the following centuries can hardly be overestimated, but it is just this division which we have to

5

criticize later from the development of physics in our time. . . . If one follows the great difficulty which even eminent scientists like Einstein had in understanding and accepting the Copenhagen interpretation of quantum theory, one can trace the roots of this difficulty to the Cartesian partition. This partition has penetrated deeply in the human mind during the three centuries following Descartes and it will take a long time for it to be replaced by a really different attitude toward the problem of reality.[3]

In one way or another we are concerned throughout this book with just that polarity: the presumably basic pole of the body-economic plus associated, subsidiary political and social institutions as being the stable terrain of man and society, and the other pole, the mental/educational/scientific/philosophical/cultural/spiritual and other associated institutions. The latter constitutes, paradoxically, the lesser although higher, more ethereal domain of man in the more misty regions of society.

Karl Marx did not discover or invent the economic basis of life. Marx took from the classical economists, especially Adam Smith, the concept that wealth is to be understood as production, as products of utility to man. The discovery of economic value and its crucial importance to human beings, said to be Adam Smith's in his *The Wealth of Nations,* is noted by Sebastian de Grazia, in his history of work and leisure, in these terms: "An act is truly productive if it takes raw material and makes it into something useful to man . . . work like this is really the beginning of wealth." And then, de Grazia comments: "The classical economists and democrats took over the idea, the anarchists found it just right, the socialists embraced it—all varieties of socialists: the communist, the Christian, utopian, and scientific."[4]

However, if God was not dead for everyone, as clearly he was for many, he had been put in his proper place. One's soul might still go to heaven—depending on where one's mind or heart had been prior to death—while one's body returned to the physical elements, but for the most part things proper to God were assigned to their category and things proper to the other parts of man were assigned to those other categories. Entire nations were of course concerned with maximizing wealth in the economic sense even when still concerned with maintaining holiness or spirituality of their empires. With time, the latter aspect faded into merely symbolic significance.

Man, in fact, had slipped into being a model of productive man. Products were pursued and used. Even if money or other forms of capital were being accumulated in the pursuit of wealth, wealth that with further commodity production and exchange could grow always larger, the name of the game had become the seeking of products—and services—for their varied present or future uses. Products were needed for survival and for pleasure, for paupers and for merchant princes. Even for the religious, God and spirit no longer inhabited most objects and products. And it seemed very clear, not mysterious at all, that some products, some production domains, were of and for economic goods and services and others were for such matters as government, philosophy, art, and the rest of the categories of needs people were assumed to have.

Marx did not invent the concepts of either wealth or productive labor, the latter also being a concept for which he thanked Adam Smith. Unlike most classical economists or philosophers and quite contrary to the then prominent group of so-called German idealists and the great Hegel himself, though, Marx did stress that economic pursuits were the *basic* pursuits. Economic institutions shaped all others more often than vice versa, even if Marx's was a broad view of society as having a set of interrelated sectors or sides, only one of them being the economic.[5]

Here is how Engels described Marx's major contribution:

Just as Darwin discovered the law of development of organic nature, so Marx discovered the law of development of human history: the simple fact, hitherto concealed by an overgrowth of ideology, that mankind must first of all eat, drink, have shelter and clothing, before it can pursue politics, science, art, religion, etc.; that therefore the production of the immediate material means of subsistence and consequently the degree of economic development attained by a given people or during a given epoch form the foundation upon which the state institutions, the legal conceptions, art and even the ideas on religion of the people concerned have been evolved, and in the light of which they must therefore be explained, instead of *vice versa,* as had hitherto been the case.[6]

Engels' own words provide us with precisely the grounds for asking whether Marxists, any more than non-Marxists, can really believe that mankind could ever have had an organization or a structure of needs such that the search for food, clothing, and shelter preceded the pursuit of politics or science. We find it impossible to imagine production of the immediate material means of subsistence in the absence of or before politics, art, religion, and even science—no matter how rudimentary. It is possible to imagine this only if one has a particular conception of such enterprises as politics, science, and economics. Such a conception is a so-called institutional conception. It is based on the premises of the existence of specific and discrete human values and of the human ability to organize value-specific projects to pursue and satisfy (more or less) these values, projects that have a suprapersonal longevity and substance. These projects are "institutions," and we intend to examine them and their premises in this book.

We are not unaware of writings by Engels, by Marx, and by some later Marxists that give importance to so-called superstructural institutions in the development and evolution of human history.[7] But we are not concerned here with questions of *relative* importance, nor are we concerned with notions of cause and effect (whether linear, nonlinear, or dialectical) among such facts or factors over time. We are concerned, rather, with the act of conceiving human life and human beings as *divisible* into such institutional domains as politics, science, art, and economics. What concerns us is the existence or nonexistence of institutions as aspects of reality. This is termed an ontological problem by professional philosophers, who, as well as ordinary people, may regard our concern as absurd on the face of it. Everyone knows how to distinguish such things, and in any event we all do so. But let us see how well or badly we do it.

Our questions now become these: How does one decide what are the referents of such sets of things as "economic" in contrast to "governmental" goods and services? Is it possible to differentiate culture or art from the social; cultural or artistic products from social or economic products? How does one know how to distinguish and separate one bundle of human values from another? This is not the usual boundary problem, in which matters often get fuzzy only in a narrow region around categorical dividing lines. It is a question for us of whether it is possible at all to make validly distinct categories, categories that are not so overlapping and multidimensional that they lose whatever distinctive meaning they may have been intended to have.

In fact, we think it is not plausible or right to do so in the manner that is nearly universal in modernity. This manner is a combination of two methods: tautological labeling—labeling something "economic" or "health-care" because it takes place within a setting already termed "economic" or "health-care"—and a kind of natural-social functionalism based on an a priori but subhuman model of man. And let us keep in mind during the following discussion that we are also concerned with the question of so-called basic (economic) versus less basic needs (such as cultural needs, etc.).

The first method, to repeat, is simply one of understanding a human action or transaction, product or service, production or consumption as economic, cultural, or whatever on the basis of its occurrence within a human setting already symbolized or labeled "economic" or whatever. If a building is termed a "factory," then its products are economic products. If a building is called a "school," then its products are education, knowledge, or information. If a building has a sign "hospital" or "theater," then the activities within are appropriately designated.

A little thought suggests that there are insurmountable difficulties in such an approach. The question that is begged, of course, is upon what basis the original labeling was done. The second method presumably answers that question, but it really does not.

The kind of natural-social functionalism of which we speak is pervasive in modernity. It is the kind of thinking that posits a living human being as a structure functioning through time. A person as a structure is a kind of object, a relatively time-invariant "thing," a thing or a thinglike system of interacting parts. Its functioning thus is understood either as that of a unitary creature with a set of distinguishable needs for different kinds of things or as that of a

9

composite creature consisting of distinguishable parts with distin-guishable needs. Satisfying the needs is a matter, in the latter instance, of identifying these parts and these things that make them function. Such a procedure is the orthodox procedure of long histor-ical standing. Identifying and distinguishing the needs of a unitary creature is an entirely different and, indeed, difficult proposition. We shall return to it later.

But since the first procedure was followed in the past and now undergirds modernity, let us try to understand it. It is the premise to which we have already referred, namely, that a person has a set of specific, discrete needs that has come to be thought of as funda-mentally a dualism. These needs are initially divisible according to the basic dual nature of human beings: humans need what animals need in order to function and also have more essentially human needs.

We have, then, the basic economic, essentially biological/animal-istic needs as well as some more specifically human need categories. The latter are those parts of man that have come to be known as, to be labeled, "religious," "artistic," and the like. This is a model of man with separable aspects. However, bluntly put, it is not legitimate, wise, useful, or good to believe that man can be so separated. Modern systems analysis has underlined the necessity to model systems as whole systems and not to think that a whole system can ever be merely a sum of parts (which parts do not actually exist as such outside the system of which they are a part). We submit that a person is precisely such a system: every *person* is an irreducible, indivisible system. Moreover, because they cannot be understood as individuals, as isolated from other persons, the system of the system of persons entails other persons. In any event, as we shall argue, a person must first of all be understood as a total person rather than a partialized, analyzed-aspect-by-aspect crea-ture.[8]

The traditional mistake is to conceive of man as having two or more parts, the one economic and concerned with bodily survival, with fuel and protection from the elements, and the other(s) of less basic needs. Let us examine the mistake that is made when, as is

10

often done, three categories of human needs are postulated. Such a model of a person assumes that the person has a body needing provisioning and protecting, a heart needing sociability and affection, and a mind needing intellectual stimulation and knowledge.

By holding the two latter sets of needs to be less basic, the model maker must mean that human life is imaginable over at least some moderate time span if the physical needs are met while the other needs are not. But we think it impossible to imagine *human* life without all three sets of needs being met (at whatever minimal levels *human* beings are understood to still exist). In other words, if human beings exist, the three categories of economic, social, and educational *are always* present. The economic is unimaginable without the other(s) if man as human being has existence. And people do exist.

Thus, if what distinguishes people from other forms of life are precisely the noneconomic aspects, needs, or values (for the moment, taking the list mentioned by Engels of politics, science, art, and religion), it is not legitimate, wise, useful, or good to believe that these are less basic, primary, or important for *people* than is the economic.[9]

But there is still another basic difficulty with the terms that presumably distinguish bundles or categories of needs. Such terms as "economic," "political," and the like refer neither to human values, human valuations, nor human experiences. These terms take their meaning from models of man that posit a set of objective needs, each need category being assigned such a term. Thus the same terms have come to be used to denote the things that presumably satisfy these needs. And these things may be anything, ranging from a hard, objective thing through a service, a human action, etc.

An assumption also exists that what people need they *value*. There is an underlying identity of value and need, an identity that we find wrong.

Needs, as the concept has developed, are objective in the sense of their being postulated from an understanding of man as a biological-mechanical system of separable parts. People are indeed treated as objects; they are treated as having a material divisibility. What is missing is a sense of the active subjectivity, the active valuational processes in which people engage as imaginative, intentional, and planning creatures.

Needs thus may be treated as discrete (although doing so does not permit of a sensible rule by which one can conclude that economic needs are more basic than various other human-need categories). Human values are more than things needed by people; they refer or should refer to human experiences. Human experiences cannot be thought of in terms of discrete needs or need categories; they are always multifaceted moments even though one or another facet may predominate. And human experiences, unlike human needs, have an intraself referent; they do not and cannot refer to a thing, to anything, that is located in space and time outside the person. Needs, however, may refer to what is needed as well as to the internal state of the person needing.

In order to begin to flesh out our sense of a total human-experiential moment as always being multifaceted, always involving a set of human needs in an integrated manner, we may ask how the action of taking a baby to the breast—or thrusting it away in rejection—should be conceived of and described. It is conventional to regard this action as only or primarily an economic action, a giving (or denying) of sustenance. It is simultaneously and, we believe, indivisibly a matter of social relations. It is recognition and affection—extended by the mother and constituting at least the first seeds of reciprocity on the part of the infant. But it is not only these two "matters" or "moments" of economics and social relations. It is also a primal political act, an act of influencing the baby by the mother.[10]

The beginning capability of the infant to affect the intended influence act is at hand; indeed, it is present already. It is present already or incipient even if the infant's participation is initially an animallike, physiological, or accidental response more than a premeditated expression of human values developed by a personal history of experiences. This aspect of the primal human moment, then, is one of politics, of governance. Whether it is already or develops into an expression and experience of benevolent or malevolent dictatorship; of paternalistic or, rather, maternalistic authoritarianism; or of underdeveloped but loving democracy will depend on the particular person(s) involved and their sentiments.

In any event, we would not withhold the label "politics" or even "government" from this primal moment although the mother and baby are not officials of an institutionally recognized governmental or state apparatus. Many other observers would locate this moment in nonpolitical, noninstitutional, or informally institutional everyday life. But our point is that the moment is distorted if understood as or assigned to the economic *or* social *or* political category.

We need to underline this point. In our conception, a human-experiential moment cannot be understood as consisting of divisible dimensions nor can any such moment, primal or not, be understood as consisting of one more essential or necessary and therefore more basic dimension and other less basic dimensions.

Perhaps it might be argued that maturation occurs just when such integral moments, such primitively primal, undifferentiated moments, break down in a process of fission into many specific, specialized moments; into the elementary particles, as it were, of working, of provisioning, of enlightening, of associating, of influencing. Indeed, as infants and then children are subjected to the activities of the divided, specialized institutions of modernity, is this not exactly what happens? Does not maturation consist precisely in subjecting children to longer, more intense experiences within the divisions of labor and life provided by the discrete institutional sectors, domains, and organizations of modernity? Is not maturity the development of modes of coordinating multiple roles, at least at the middle and upper levels of modern societies?

Our answer is in the negative. Despite appearances, this is not what happens. It is impossible. It is impossible because *discrete institutions do not exist*.

2

The Modern
Manufactured Reality

In the second part of this chapter we shall give the basis for our assertion that discrete institutions do not exist. To prepare that basis we must elaborate on why the false identity of needs and values has contributed to the murkiness of much of the discussion about the pros and cons of the modern consumer society. Hierarchically partialized individuals are not only people in special occupational roles. People as consumers seem particularly partialized. They are limited to acts of consumption and seemingly are related to each other only by the ability of money to pass from hand to hand or from computerized account to computerized account or to penetrate the dividing walls of institutionalized and subinstitutionalized sectors of society. When Marx spoke of "commodity fetishism," he did not mean merely that commodities constituted the fabric of organized life with the development of capitalism, although this was true. He meant that nonhuman commodities and their monetary values substituted for and symbolized the human relations that led to their existence and would determine their fate.

People as consumers seem particularly individualized as well. Each one, with his or her hierarchy of consumer orientations, is able to speak out, often in a competitive fashion. Money is always the final claimant. What is often termed the ''consumer society'' also means a very commercialized society.

Critics of consumerism speak of false needs that are created by giant multinational corporations with the assistance of their advertising specialists. Real needs are presumably displaced or submerged by these artificially created needs. But what are the *real needs*—the ''true needs''—that such critics imply? Is it true that what people have come to value are not their authentic human needs? To many people there seems to be a serious discrepancy between values and needs. The question is an important one because upon its answer rests various proposals for reform or even radical utopian transformation. Moreover, if the question is approached properly we may learn something very important about how thinking has been shaped in modernity and how it might be reshaped to the benefit of everyone. We can begin to understand how people organized in so-called institutions are concerned not with human values but with something different: needs of people not as *human* beings but merely as living creatures.

The proper approach to the question of authentic versus artificial human needs is to pose another set of prior questions: What is the general relationship between the two, between values and needs? Is the relationship one of cause and effect? Does one imply the other? Are they identical terms?

We think it will help very much to reserve the term ''needs'' for something related to a person at the infrahuman, object level. People encompass that level; they are objectifiable. But a person is also a subjective subject and, as such, has values. Values may be so consistent and stable through time that we can locate them in a present (or in a past) period of time and say that people ''have'' (or ''had'') X, Y, and/or Z values. Needs do not entail, encompass, or integrate values. Values entail needs. Values encompass needs.

Values integrate needs. Needs are integral to values, but the opposite is not the case. Values, valuable human experiences, are forged from and involve needs but are more than needs per se, while needs are specifiable without reference to *human* experiences.

Earlier we made the comment that it is impossible to imagine human life without at least three sets of needs (economic, social, and educational) being met, with the consequence that one set of needs could not be viewed as more basic than another. All are necessary, and each is insufficient.

We now suggest that it is possible to speak of the needs of people, of the economic and other categories of needs of people, *as if* one need could exist without the others; *as if,* that is, people could be treated as economic people, as social people, etc. These, of course, are not models of persons, of human beings, but of partialized and unreal human beings.

This kind of partialization is precisely what people do when they refer to or think about institutions. Apparently, we now have a basis for distinguishing institutions. But we said that discrete institutions do not exist; they cannot exist. To understand the nature of what does exist, we must now define "values" more explicitly.

"Values" are ordinary or extraordinary human experiences toward which or away from which people are oriented (i.e., prepared to move). Or, from the vantage point of the person moving through time, values can be happening, they may be regarded as actions of valuation. Values remain valuable future experiences, but they also become valuable current experiences.

Values are at the everyday level of human life. By this we mean several things. We mean that values refer to human experiences. Values refer to experiences of people as total persons. Values refer to total persons whose communicative interactions are constituted by subjectively shaped moments of which needs are an integral aspect. By this we mean that human needs are a kind of raw material for human values. They are objects that subjective man integrates not consciously, not by design, not by rational decision, but automatically and spontaneously due to the nature of human beings. People do this in a manner or form shaped by their particular social history and always with their personal stamp. These personal stamps may be very similar to or different from those of others, that is, very standardized or very idiosyncratic, depending on both history and the particular person.

The needs themselves, whether for hard physical material or soft caresses, words, or even glances; for the workings of strong, sheltering objects or for less tangible information; are conceptualizable as divisible. They have been separated into various numbers and kinds of categories by psychologists, philosophers, and plain people throughout history. They have the property of divisibility because as the stuff, the raw material, of such conceptualizations, they are approachable precisely through parts of man, through partialized systems of analysis, through models of composite people, which really are models of infra-, extra-, or nonhuman creatures.

These partialized needs, however, as we shall demonstrate, are integral to encompassing human-valuational, human-experiential moments. They are incorporated, encapsulated, or fused into moments that are prismatic in the sense that these needs coexist like the multiple facets of a prism. Depending on various things, probably including emotional states, a human experience may seem to have an artistic or aesthetic facet or at other times a social, associational, or other facet predominating, but there is always more than one facet present. We shall say more about this in a while.

At this human-experiential level, which we term one of everyday life, then, we mean that persons exist in their totality, in their holistic human sense. They do not exist as partialized people, as professionals or experts or role players defined in terms of any particular need-satisfying enterprise. Nor do they exist as people whose primary identity results from the particular piece of fragmented social space (housewives, students, retired people, etc.) into which modernity has been manufactured and mapped. At least there, despite appearances to the contrary, total persons exist.

In everyday life people are not only total persons; they are also total *social* persons. By this we mean to emphasize that no matter how unique each person is, no one really resembles the "individual," the abstract and solitary creature of so much social science.

The model of man as individual was given birth to by philosophers creating fantasies about man living as a social hermit in some kind of romanticized and impossible state of nature. This concept has facilitated the construction of models of people that stress functional needs of abstract, analytically divided individuals rather than human-experiential values of more total persons, forged in the crucible of interpersonal relations.

No matter how long and lonely is a particular person's solitary task or condition, it is an experience that has its significance, its "functional" significance, in terms of those communicative interactions that have occurred with other people—even if the current experience itself is a personal religious (one-person-to-God) or artist-creating-alone experience.

Persons have experiences that are shaped by them as particular persons, that are stamped by them personally. No person's experience can quite be another's experience; every person must only imagine rather than experience precisely what another person experiences. But the ever-present potential for closing the gap between two persons or reducing it almost to its vanishing point comes from the very general human ability to understand each other's and one's own values. People participate in commonly understood experiences as total persons, subject to the particular historical peculiarities of language, customs, and rites that may, of course, make for barriers to such communicative interactions outside the given group. Human values are socially forged values no matter how idiosyncratic a single person's values may become.

By "understanding" we mean not a partialized, solely intellectual comprehension but the intellectual and emotional empathy that characterizes all human communicative interaction, no matter how cool or phlegmatic the emotional facet may be.[1] Nor do we intend to suggest that people become less than total persons if they should find themselves infused with feelings of rejection or strangeness should they encounter a group performing with a communication system that blocks them from participating or understanding what is going on. Total persons may have different or even conflicting human values.

Needs, on the other hand, have referents to analytically partialized persons. Concretely, needs are statements of what inputs, supplies, or provisions are necessary for a person modeled as a functioning, complex creature at other than the fully personal (interpersonal) level of human experience. The inputs are necessary for the person to function at all as well as the causal model suggests is potentially possible. Needs, in other words, are requirements for inputs to people. If they are not satisfied there results either functioning at a level below the maximum permitted by the model or malfunctioning (including the possibility of total breakdown).

Would it not be possible to imagine a functional model of a person such that certain human experiences constituted the necessary inputs for best functioning and, consequently, those inputs could be both values and needs? For example, can we not imagine a model that posits the necessity of children receiving a certain amount of love and affection, that is, as a necessary input, for their best (most healthy, etc.) functioning as adult persons? Would not love be an example of an input that was both a need and a value?[2]

If the model is developed at the human-experiential level, it cannot conceptualize children in this mechanical fashion, with love being considered merely an "input," a cause of a consequent output. In fact, the example says nothing about love as a value of children, but treats love as a value of those adults who are providing it to the children. Love in this example involves, as values always do, outputs "put out" by others while the recipients presumably have the need for this output. There are two different meanings of love in this example: its meaning for those expressing it and its meaning for those to whom it is addressed.

Much confusion would be avoided if different terms were used in such cases. In the present instance, if the parents were doing the loving and the children were merely taking it in, another term, such as "emotional nourishment," might be better used in speaking of what the children received. They would be provisioned or serviced by the adults while the latter were experiencing love.

However, suppose the children were also engaging reciprocally with the adults in such a process. Then, indeed, "loving" would be an appropriate word to describe the human values involved (although even better words than "love" might be in order). But whether the adults alone were loving or both were so experiencing, the provision of emotional nourishment, that is, the servicing of such a need, would also be happening as an aspect or facet of the experiential moment. Because "needs" refers to a model of a person with multiple but partialized categories, other facets, including the economic sheltering and fueling processes, the aesthetic, etc., are also present.

If in this instance the children were not themselves loving reciprocally, what human experience were they having? The children's human-experiential moments might be even at the opposite value pole of hate, the inversion of love, and thus be a kind of emotional starvation or distortion. Or they might be nonreciprocating and entirely outside the experience of loving (or hating). Loving as the experiential moment may exist for someone while the other person experiences something quite different or finds need satisfaction in such a disguise that he or she does not even recognize the love for what it is.

We emphasize that values entail needs but needs do not entail particular kinds of experiential values. If "love" were a word reserved for a certain kind of positive human-experiential value, we might want to say that all human beings have a need for love. But that would not be a useful or a true statement. Think of a person whose sexual activities always involve making use of a prostitute in a mechanical, nonaffectionate way. We would not say love was involved in such a case even if the person were satisfying sexual needs. If we said such a person should love, should have a need for love, we might be quite right or wise. We would be quite wrong if we thought such a person was not a total person having a human experience when the person was with the prostitute. As we shall say again later, even unpleasant, degrading, or distorted human experiences are human. Even if we do not have sufficient language to describe them properly, we do not clarify things by reverting to the language of, or thinking of them as only, partialized needs.

At a truly human experiential level, love might be conceived of as being produced and consumed simultaneously. Actually, the economist's idea of needs, especially basic needs, as being the ultimate basis for product demand is quite appropriate for the economist's purposes, but the idea of human values is not an economic idea. It is inexpressible or only badly expressed in the language of economists for reasons that we shall mention in a while. Unfortunately, we have a poverty of language for speaking of the total moments that comprise happenings and encounters at the human-experiential level.

As in the present example of love, all human values at the experiential level involve on the part of at least one person a relationship to another that is explicable by a coordinate system that assumes a giving and a taking, receiving, or getting. But even if the relationship is a reciprocal one, the language of exchange is inappropriate because such language misstates what the actor's motive is as well as what happens to each person in the relationship.

Thus it is that we find in the so-called behavioral sciences such ideas as the value-maximizing model of man.[3] The confusion between values and needs, between *human* models of man as subject and *scientific* models of man as object, is great. The biological fact that persons are mortal, that their time as living creatures on this earth is limited, leads into the trap of assuming that therefore people are concerned with time, with limited time, as such. One of the sacred beliefs of our society to which we referred at the outset is the seemingly self-evident belief that time is of value, that it is scarce and thus entails costs. Time is indeed a human need, but it is never a value as such.

We have heard from or about Karl Marx several times so far. Let us hear from a man who while not a contributor to original political thought has been rightly acclaimed as someone who speaks with a very clear voice and does, we believe, present the central principles of the American political economy. This person is Robert Dahl, a political scientist, who put the matter of time as a ''crucial'' value in these terms: ''Let us accept the palpable fact that your own time is limited. . . . In its interactions with space, time compels exclusion. . . . When I write, I cannot play tennis. Thus, time insists upon sacrifice. . . . Time is of value . . . and scarce . . . [and has] costs.''[4] Running through American liberalism and conservatism as well as through Soviet and European Marxism is the notion that values are scarce, time being merely an obvious example of a supposedly scarce value. In the nature of things, in the nature of nature, people find themselves in a situation in which sacrifice and effort are necessary to satisfy basic and less basic needs. Value generally derives from the fact that human effort is required to wrest a living from nature. It is not a matter of receiving manna from heaven. Even people long ago who gathered things to eat from trees or hunted animals had to expend effort. For the classical economists as for Marx, wealth emerges from work. If there are any true needs, then, may they not be located in these basic considerations?

Listen again to Dahl:

> Rationality, efficiency, economy are all different ways of speaking about essentially the same elementary thing. Rationality speaks to the unarguable notion that it is always desirable to obtain more of your values than fewer. Efficiency emphasizes the idea of gaining more output, or, if you prefer, more of what you value, for less input, that is, for less cost to what you value. Economy stresses that many of the things you value are scarce and that by wasting these scarce resources you reduce the total value of what you attain.[5]

Without denying a universal existential anxiety rooted in human mortality, we must deny Dahl's ''palpable fact'' that time is limited. Yes, it is in the nature of a person to live ''exclusively'' in the sense of not being able to do many or all things at once. Nor can we deny that an economist may develop a theory about ''opportunity costs'' paid by people who do some things rather than other things. But *the* important fact is that time is limited only to the extent that people *make* of time such a limit; of time as requiring sacrifice, as scarce, as costly, and as of value per se.

Do we say the same thing about food? About clothing? About shelter? Yes, we do. The opportunity costs of the economist may or may not be costs felt and paid by people as people. They may be costs calculated by an observer, whether or not the human subjects feel or pay them. They may be costs the economist makes a part of the model of people as economic people, as people in their animal or biological aspects. Whether such costs are human costs—whether people make the production, saving, or consumption of goods and services of value—depends on specific persons in specific historical contexts.

But do not all people at all times and in all conditions have as the basic or primary values those material goods and services essential for survival, i.e., the economic values? As we have said already, no, they do not. We know from people who have preferred death in battle or suicide to survival that it is not a permanent and universal law for such economic values to be primary. These exceptions disprove any statement that it is human *nature* for such things to be basic and primary in the sense of *always* having predominant human value.

Apart from the patriots, heroes, crusaders, and fools, the question remains, of course, as to whether or not minimally intelligent people are rationally, efficiently, and economically oriented in Dahl's sense. In fact, the idea that at least the proverbial reasonable man obviously and always wants more output for less input seems eminently sensible, but it is wrong. People may be said to have needs for efficiency or for efficiencies of various kinds, but it would be wrong to say that they obviously and always want to maximize values, that is, what to minimize costs (minimize *their* inputs, efforts, energy, etc., while maximizing *their* outputs). At the *human-experiential* level, people may satisfy themselves, their values, by maximizing their inputs, thereby giving more to other people than they get. (Again, it is a large assumption that quantification can substitute at all for qualities of relationships which are beyond such econometric or engineering concepts as economy or efficiency.)

Needs, then, are located in reference to parts of a person who is conceptualized as divisible. Such analytic partializability results in lists usually of broad categories of needs, lists often varying considerably in their number of categories. It is in just this context that people may debate about which needs are more and which are less basic. And they may engage in what we would consider equally sterile debate about true and false needs and about real and pseudo values of human beings.

Such an approach to a total person, that of analyzing a person into parts to which are attached discrete needs, cannot produce a total person by a reverse process of addition of parts. It cannot because the total person must be conceptualized in terms of molar person-to-person (and person-to-self) experiences. Nor can a total person result from a systems approach that models a person as a complex of needs conceived as parts or subsystems in dynamic interaction. This method does not and cannot produce a total person with values because any system must be modeled as properly in whole as in its parts or subsystems.

The values of a person cannot be regarded in any sense as parts of the person, nor do they refer to parts of the person. Rather they refer to the states or moments, to the experiences, of the total person. The moments of a person are understandable and specifiable as moments in which he or she, the entire person, participates and experiences what only people can experience. At least, only people can speak about such experiences. And speech is vital for imagining: for planning and for making ethics and morality, perhaps the most essential of all the qualities of human being-ness.

Human-experiential moments are multifaceted. Sometimes we use the word "multidimensional," but the latter word has a misleading connotation of somehow distinguishable, separable dimensions. The facets of which we speak may include needs and the structures and processes that constitute the human-need apparatus, but they include them only at a distance. Needs are not recognizable as such when embedded as facets of values. By this we mean that provision of food, fuel, or energy for the body, for example, if regarded as an economic need of man, is a kind of thrust involved in a human dining process. But the human experience of dining involves other facets, such as humanly (socially) developed tastes and tasting, being with other people, feeling secure and not threatened by enemies, etc.

Human experience embodies needs in such a manner that the needs are not distinct elements. They are involved, as we said, but are integrated into the human-experiential moments. If they are observable and measurable, they are so as infrahuman, biological, physical, chemical, or whatever the specialty doing the observing or measuring, but not as human phenomena as such.

Even the physical tensions associated with hunger may not be involved in dining if a person is fortunate. If such bodily needs are present, they may not be noticed. Even if they are present and are noticed, they may not be assessed as a distinct part of a dining process. If, however, the hunger is extremely strong and becomes the solitary thrust of the person, that is, if the person is concerned only with relieving the hunger pains, we have an example of a person reduced at least momentarily to an infrahuman or extrahuman, animallike condition in human experiencing. A person may savor food to the point of being known as a gourmet or a glutton, but concentration is neither animallike nor single-faceted, as an economic sense of eating suggests. At the limit, then, man may cross the edge of humanity into subhuman, animallike states, but ordinarily death rescues man from such entrapment before very long.

Let us be clear. Even brutes, sadists, the worst Nazis are persons whose values are horrible but who are not usually characterized by a constant, single-faceted value, as a hungry, human-killing animal may be characterized. When such persons act as they do, they are appropriately thought of as animallike persons or, better, as vicious-animal-like people. Our effort is not to romanticize but to try to understand even them as whole persons rather than as the fragments that modernity seems to have fabricated as their fate and apparent reality.

We may now speak to the matter of how to approach the aforementioned question of whether in modern society there are some real human needs that have been engulfed by artificial needs, some true needs engulfed by false needs. Has the consumer society created such a situation? Our answer is that such a question is properly addressed to the vast array of scientific disciplines that have developed with the specialized division of labor in modernity. It may be answered, and variously, by specialists in biology, in physical chemistry, in neurology, in nutrition, and in the other fields and subfields. The question can be approached by positing normals (norms) of functioning, including superb functioning, in regard to the various matters into which we can and do analyze people and their organs/parts. Then we can inquire into such things as how many Coca-Colas cause teeth to decay prematurely or creativity to occur.

It is in such a context that there may well be general scientific (as well as commonsense) agreement that economic efficiency is a universal requirement for furthering the physical survival of living creatures, including people. But in our effort to de-economize the most influential current models of persons, we must immediately add that there are equally important universal requirements having to do with other than economic needs. Nor are most people, including economists, particularly concerned with such matters as efficiency by the human survivors in the aftermath of a nuclear holocaust or other ecological-human disaster.

But the significant question to us is another. This would be the question of whether human beings have developed false or artificial rather than true or authentic human values. How many, to what extent, where, and how permanently do people pursue false values? Or do people have false or pseudo experiences? If we mean by "false" harmful to the person in any single system or aspect sense or even to the whole person's physical or mental health, then the question is one of economics, psychology, or medical science. If, however, by "false" or "artificial" we mean "bad" and by "true" or "authentic" we mean "good," which is just what we do mean, then we have returned the question to its properly human ethical foundation.

Such questions are never only ethical. They always involve dimensions of biological or physical functioning. But as value questions, they require an approach very different from the approach to functional questions concerning needs or parts of man. The former require, but the latter do not, a model of total persons, their human experiences, and the unescapable moral dimensions of such experiences, although the last may not be prominent features of the experiences or a predominant concern to the person posing the value question.

So, too, are scientific approaches to the many questions that may be posed about the needs of people often complicated by the fact that people themselves, people as objects, are subjective, valuing creatures and, hence, not as easily understood or studied as are nonhuman creatures or physical stuff. Scientists themselves are human, and their own models may be shaped by their values, a matter now often recognized although not easily handled. And often at the level of pure neurology or physiology or "behavioral" psychology (studies of perceptions, of people as biological creatures, of people as animals only, etc.), models and assessments of the needs of people may vary and even conflict. In other words, specialized science does not ensure a conflictfree study of man, while a more holistic approach to total persons cannot be even attempted without immediately encountering not merely lightly value-laden but heavily value-impregnated human experiences.

Before addressing the aforementioned question about whether people are pursuing bad experiences or values in today's so-called consumer society, we will extend the examination of needs and values a bit. Then we shall be in a position to see how the question of institutions and their asserted nonexistence relates to the matter of false values.

We have argued so far that the traditional approach to people as composite entities consisting of segments is not the appropriate way to understand people as people. There is often an identity made between human needs and human values which we suggested is illegitimate and confusing, to say the least. The authoritative model in modernity is actually a three-category model, with a similar confusion and equally misleading results. And it is the model that directly underlies the modern understanding of institutions.

Persons, in this authoritative model, are understood as consisting of various kinds and categories of needs, the list varying with the model builder. These needs may be regarded as very specific and concrete or quite diffuse, even, at the latter extreme, merely as dispositions. Now, such a model postulates another phase or stage, sometimes merely a reflection of the needs and sometimes a kind of intermediate level of a person distinct from the underlying needs. Various words, including "aptitudes," "faculties," "capabilities," "abilities," "skills," and "talents," have been used to designate this latter stage or level. The next stage or level may be regarded as the one we have termed "values," with such words also used as "desires," "wants," "aspirations," and "interests." But unlike our definition of "values," in the dominant modern model they may be as discrete as the underlying faculties and (possibly even more underlying) needs.

The model of the person that emerges is that of a human being whose attributes in regard to the various intermediate categories, let us call them "talents," range from no or low through very high potential. Or they may be regarded as varying from primitive through normal to excellent or exceptional. Or the various dimensions may be regarded as ranging from undeveloped through average to highly developed. In any event, whether the talents are or are not subsumed under the concept of needs, they underlie, support, and constitute the ingredients of interests. And institutions are those places and spaces wherein people are provided with the stuff necessary for expressing their talents (and/or needs) and with the opportunities to express their interests. Institutions, then, are required by the model that posits such categories of human composition, competence, and essential functioning. Although models conflict as to the universality or potentiality of human beings regarding such need/talent categories and the degree of institutional satisfaction of existing or potential interests, they agree on understanding institutions as specific to the major categories of such needs/talents/interests, which are by their nature as discrete as their corollary institutions.

All such models rest on the possibility of distinguishing sets of categories of talents (or needs) and related interests (or values). Otherwise there would be little possibility of understanding how appropriately specialized institutions can perform coherently and consistently with the talents/interests with which they are especially concerned.

The safest ground for such a categorization is to find in people and in nature, that is, in human nature, a set of discrete talent categories of a transhistorical, transcultural character. Interests may be expected to be shaped by history and culture, but aptitudes—in their fundamental aspects if not in their details—should rest on and be rooted in the essential human nature of persons. In other words, the model gains credibility to the extent that it rests on definitions that are technical, that partake of objective physical or biological science rather than of subjective social science. The model suggests, then, that needs shape values, innate abilities determine interests, natural aspects of people dominate human experiences or at least precede them in personal as in historic time.

There is a crucial experiment that may be performed in imagination if not in another reality to probe the validity of this person-institution model. One cannot physically dissect a person to see if the basic need and/or talent categories are actually present. A person does not reveal such aptitudes from a postmortem perspective. The talent may be a disposition whose various ingredients, structures, and mechanisms are entirely unknown, at least to modern science. More important, the evidence of a talent, an ability, a faculty, or whatever the term is knowable only from its exercise, from what is made or produced and/or used or consumed in the course of the particular activity. Whether the category refers to music and art or to shelter and food, it is the objects presumably distinguishing different categories of activities, talents, or capabilities that permit one to conclude that the particular categories do exist. Such categories exist in the persons and institutions presumably organized around object-specific activities.

The crucial experiment is to examine, say, music and houses to see if in their different natures as objects we find an objective basis for distinguishing their parental cultural and economic classifications. The reader may think this is a nonsensical pursuit. It is not nonsensical to look for the basis upon which to distinguish institutions. So far we have argued that the traditional model of people as composite entities consisting of parts is not the appropriate way to proceed to understand them. A person with postulated talents (aptitudes, faculties, skills, capabilities, or abilities) that correspond to so-called needs and with interests (desires, wants, aspirations) that correspond to so-called values is just such a model, and it seems to be the authoritative model underlying the development and existence of institutions.

Various models may and do conflict as to the universality of the need/value categories, but in all models the person is understood as a partializable individual with need/value-specific institutions providing people with the stuff for their talents (needs) and opportunities for the expression of their interests (values). Why do we find this kind of model inappropriate?

Let us start our examination with institutions—one cultural or artistic and another economic—that are supposedly distinguishable and specific to quite different kinds of talents/interests. The reader may think this is a nonsensical pursuit—looking for the basis upon which to distinguish institutions that are obviously distinguishable. Is it not obvious that the cultural institution, wherein people have their needs for music met and/or express their talents for making music or even for being listeners at concerts, is easily distinguishable from, let us say, the economic institution of house building? Making music and making houses; producing and consuming music and producing and consuming houses. Making music is not building a house and vice versa. We seem to have a clear example of distinguishable institutions—or do we?

We are not engaged in the aforementioned tautological exercise of saying that what takes place in a building termed a ''concert hall'' or ''theater'' is music, hence we have a cultural institution rather than a house-building or house-inhabiting economic or social institution. Nor are we engaged in solving the aforementioned boundary problem, that is, the problem of locating a person or the person's activities within one or another of two institutions. If institutions are discrete, if they are separable in any real sense, persons may be within two (or more) institutions simultaneously but only in the space wherein the institutions overlap. We are not concerned here with such intersections. Our concern is with the central portions of institutions, that is, with parts or areas that seem clearly distinguishable.

Unless institutions are centrally distinguishable, not only are they not discrete by definition, but also they cannot have the meaning ordinarily attributed to them. The aforementioned authoritative model of a person with various discrete sets of aptitudes or capabilities and of society with companion institutions for the exercise of such talents, although seemingly sensible, fails if our imaginary experiment results in our finding no objective or technical basis for distinguishing human music making and human house building. This is precisely the result although initially it might not seem to be so.

Suppose people working in the house-construction industry try to use their hammer or saw in a music-making fashion while on the job. Even if they disregard or minimize the fact of their economic institutional identity and the consequences of their noninstitutional or other institutional (music-making) activities to the (economic) construction of the house, it is likely that other people higher in the latter organizational hierarchy will treat them as construction workers rather than as musicians. If such "deviants" persist in their on-the-job music making, they may finally have to choose between making a career of playing building tools as musical instruments on the stage or playing in their free time. Otherwise they will face the dangers that institutional deviants often encounter in a society that desires institutional discreteness and clarity and the efficiencies that flow therefrom. At bottom everyone knows that music and houses are different and the difference is in the nature of the world.

We have then, it would seem, a simple and real basis for distinguishing such institutions. To repeat, this basis is the difference in the nature of the objects (e.g., music and houses) of concern to participants, at least to informed and influential leaderships, and the correlated differences in the human activities of object production and of object consumption or use.

Unfortunately, such a simple basis quickly proves to be unreal or unreliable. And it is unreliable even before we inquire into the wisdom of attributing to participants in a set of activities the meaning and significance (e.g., cultural or economic) presumably inherent in the objects of such activities. Objects and object-related activities are not self-evidently distinguishable; it is not a technical matter or one embedded in the objective nature of the world for music and houses to be distinguishable. If and when they are distinguishable, it is always according to human decision and convention.

Is music definable technically without reference to historically varying social subjectivities? No, it is impossible. It is impossible not only given what passes for music in the range of primitive to complex societies and what historically has happened to the definition of music (including current electronic music) only in the countries of Western Europe. It is impossible also because technical vocabularies are themselves necessarily also firmly connected to so-called natural languages, which are obviously socially forged and historically variable.

Music is not definable without reference to *human* beings. However technical a definition is offered in terms of acoustics, other branches of physics, anatomy, and physiology (relative to hearing and the ear), mankind demands some further human connotations no matter how difficult such definitions may be. And these definitions must be human-experiential in character. For some societies and people certain sounds are music, for others they are noise, and for still others they are nothing at all.

Perhaps houses as objects and house building as an activity are more easily definable in technical terms? May not houses, perhaps more simply than music, be defined in terms of their function for human beings, that is, providing shelter, providing protection for the body, providing a material means of subsistence? May not houses be good examples of objects that are naturally scarce and also intimately connected to the natural and very basic human survival need for shelter?

If houses can be approached in that manner, then the capability or talent of people for producing houses as well as the capability or talent for inhabiting them, for using or consuming them, would seem to be established. And it would seem appropriate to proceed in that manner. Is it not clear that a house *is* a house even if fashions and styles of housing change over time? Alas, it is not clear.

It is not clear for precisely the same reason that it is not clear what

32

constitutes music to people unless one takes into account the human culture. Even as the human world shrinks and an international style of housing becomes more prevalent, we are still not dealing with a definitional matter that has an objective, technical, valuefree quality. And it is not important that music does not have the kind of hard objectivity that houses do, because as Marx himself insisted, a product may come into being, exist (although perhaps for a shorter period of time), and represent the result of labor "even if not solidified in a thing." It is a major misconception among many Marxists that the crux of a product for Marx was its solid physical materiality. Products, including artistic and musical products, were indeed material just as language was substantial "in the form of agitated layers of air, sound."[6] Indeed, for Marx "language is practical consciousness."[7]

The problem lies precisely where it did when we tried to examine the essential objectively real needs of human beings. When we try to understand the essential aspects of objects or of the activities that produce or consume them, we find that they have meaning only because people are human; people are subjective subjects. As subjective subjects, they have the capability to objectify themselves and each other. And the purpose has often been good rather than bad. Is it not good to create a housing industry that can concentrate on that aspect or need (shelter) that humans share with other animals and produce, efficiently and effectively, as many houses as possible?

Of course, barracks and prisons are forms of shelter and housing, but we are not advocating "inhuman" housing for most people. Of course the houses must be designed so that they take into account some of the differences between the animal called man and other animals. These are matters of politics; of social relations; indeed, even of ethics and aesthetics.

Neither bourgeois nor Marxist economists think that because something is of objective material hardness or even because so-called self-regulating market conditions exist, such a matter is thereby removed from the subjective considerations that determine both in broad outline and in particular details the workings of such economic institutions (or subinstitutions) as a housing industry. Adam Smith's "invisible hand" works only if human hands and intentions are operating, regardless of whether consequences be intended or unintended. And Karl Marx's commodity fetishism, a hallmark of capitalism, is analogous to Smith's magic market in the sense that it refers to human relations that have become hidden behind and subservient to seemingly subjective relations among objects.[8]

To repeat what appears to be an obvious point but requires repetition, housing for people is never merely a matter of shelter for bodies. It is always shelter for bodies and more. Even so-called quantitative housing questions involve qualitative, subjective, human preferences. Animals may have little or no choice regarding their shelter, taking it where they can or being programmed instinctually to construct it in certain ways. But when people consider such matters as volumes and sizes and numbers of houses—the stuff of urban planning—it is evident that we cannot even begin to remove the matter of subjective preferences.[9]

If people considered houses to be only shelter for their bodies, perhaps we would define houses more simply and functionally as objects—of use, of utility, of consumption—than we can music. But they do not and we cannot. When people are considered potential customers or consumers of houses, they are not only objectified and treated impersonally, merely as people with money to spend. They are also treated in a particular subjective mode, as impotent, as without rights or abilities to participate in the decision-making process of building houses.

Acceptance of such *political* impotence is signaled positively by the purchase or rental of the houses by a sufficient number of people. It is of no consequence that justifications can be offered for acquiescence in such a relationship of dominance and subordination. The fact is that houses in every stage from design through production and construction to consumption are more than merely economic objects; they are also prime political objects. They are the stuff of politics in a most immediate and central sense. Regardless of conventional institutional thinking and such dichotomies as private and public, houses are political as much as they are economic. It is only on the rare occasion when the homeless protest or occupy vacant housing that we have this sense of houses being political rather than merely economic products, having profound political as well as economic and aesthetic utilities, forms, and meanings.

If, then, a house is not merely a shelter, an economic object, can a house-construction *industry* be understood as merely an economic institution or subinstitution? Not in terms of the nature of the objects of concern, that is, not in terms of houses being specific to particular human categories of needs or capabilities of users. But might not house building be first and foremost an economic institution in the sense of the activities performed by the producers? Might not houses as objects obtain their significance as economic from the perspective of those participating in production?

People who so participate do so for one simple reason: to make money. If this is not the only reason, it is the primary reason. If it is not the primary reason for all people, it is primary for the vast bulk of humanity. If given the choice, who would work? So goes the syllogism that undergirds and produces the idea of economic activities and, hence, economic institutions. Can anyone really disagree with such a model of human motivation?

The first difficulty is that every one of these statements admits of exceptions. Making money is not the only reason for working on the part of all people. It may not even be the primary reason for some people. For how many may it be not even a subsidiary reason? How many people regard making money not as a *reason* for working at all and thus not as a means to other ends—not to speak of money not being an end in itself? Such people might even regard the moneymaking aspect of work as an inescapable consequence, as natural as breathing. Among such people, as well as others who think differently, there might indeed be people who would work even if given the possibility of not having to do so.

A conventional economic model of human motivation is clearly not a very strong one. It does not suggest something about the nature of all people and, hence, is a less secure foundation than it might be for determining whether particular sets of activities are economic.

Perhaps, however, we should not speak of motives or interests but simply of consequences associated with certain sets of activities.

Perhaps economic activities are those activities that produce incomes for the participants. The incomes represent life-sustaining goods and services and may be in the form of money, of credits, or in kind. But now we have the problem of the meaning of "life-sustaining." Can life be sustained only with food, drink, clothing, and shelter? May activities of love making also generate life-sustaining goods and services? We do not here refer to commercialized prostitution.

Indeed, perhaps homemakers should be thought of as workers deserving money wages or salaries, but does this mean every human activity that generates income in the form of life-sustaining goods and services is economic rather than something else? What would follow, and indeed does follow for those who take a broadly economic view and see all human capabilities as well as all or nearly all associated interests as having utility for the person engaging therein, is the elimination of the problem of categorization of needs, talents, or interests of people as well as of institutions. One and all are economic—whatever else of a subsidiary nature they may be. In fact, this is a solution adopted by both economists of capitalism and Karl Marx himself. Marx went the additional step of seeing some institutions as substructural and others as superstructural. In a confusing kind of terminology, the former then became the economic and the latter, the others, the political, the artistic, the ideological, etc. But Marx's model of person and society was of person as the producer (and consumer) and society as a set of productive institutions with a few marginal ones only of pleasure.

It was also Marx, though, who offered the central reason for not being able to use objects, whether or not solidified in things, as the criterion for distinguishing human needs, talents, or interests. Marx's model of human beings was both narrow and broad. It was narrowly economistic in the sense of seeing persons as engaged in *production* (distribution, exchange, and consumption) in all domains. It was broad in the senses both of understanding persons as existing and producing in a wide range of domains and of understanding persons as essentially in and of history. Persons are profoundly subjective in their understanding and development of their needs, capabilities, and interests; they are deeply influenced by history, especially by the human relations of production of goods and services, just as they themselves influence history.

Goods and services themselves, the objects of our concern here, were conceived by Marx at least sometimes as not inherently having an objective meaning. In fact, an object produced—a product— could not attain its meaning as a product until it was consumed. A product was not even a product until consumed. Contrary to all who thought or still think that Marx was portraying objectively and scientifically the movement of real objects in the lawful workings of capitalism, Marx was actually portraying the behavior of very subjective people. People by and in their subjectivity gave objective status to products. They gave them values that could become actualized only if people performed in an objectified manner, only if they performed in the manner promised or compelled by the power relations existing among those who inherited or acquired narrowly circumscribed roles in the production process stamped by the (then) modern division of labor. And subjectivity remained a crucial feature of otherwise seemingly hard, objective products.

Listen to the middle-aged Marx of *Die Grundrisse*: "A railway on which no trains run, hence which is not used up, not consumed, is a railway *only potentially*, and *not in reality*." (Emphasis added.)[10] Again, "A garment becomes a real garment only in the act of being worn; a house where no one lives in in fact no real house; thus the product, unlike a mere natural object, proves itself to be, *becomes* a product only through consumption."[11]

On the other hand, Marx himself was a man of his own institutional, philosophic, and linguistic age, at least in part. For example, he made the aforementioned exception for "mere natural object[s]." He thus seemed to think that somehow in nature there were objects that had, per se, an inherent, scientific, suprahuman "natural," indeed, objective, meaning. His simultaneous sensitivity to the importance of subjective meanings and significances of basic categories and unconscious commitment to a sense of obvious, commonsensical, and self-evident reality of institutionally distinct objects is suggested in his comments on how production also affects consumption: "The object of art—like every other product—creates a public which is sensitive to art and enjoys beauty. Production thus not only creates an object for the subject, but also a subject for the object."[12] In so few words Marx beautifully captures the idea of dynamic interaction regarding matters often thought of as more separated. Yet in the same breath he uses the conventional institutional division between objects of art and objects not of art!

Although many if not most self-proclaimed Marxists would scream with indignation at the thought, we find that Marx's sense of the essentiality of personal and interpersonal practices in providing meanings for objects, at least for humanly made objects, even the physically substantial, presumably objective world of objects, was thoroughly historical and subjective. There has been a debate among Marxists as to whether Marx was more a cultural anthropologist or historian, or a hard scientist or political economist type (and as to whether a young, soft Marx, concerned with human alienation, differed from a mature, hardened Marx, concerned with the impersonal, objective laws of systems). We find one Marx, and this one a person of great acumen when it came to such matters as understanding how much his modernity was a manufactured reality in so many fundamental regards. He had a penetrating sense that underlying seemingly suprapersonal objects of all kinds were human beings and very human relations, as we shall see. Yet the same Karl Marx was a man of double consciousness in a specific sense of that term, as we shall also indicate in the next chapter.

Our point should now be made. We must conclude that neither objects of human activity nor the human activity itself is sufficient to provide a simple basis for distinguishing categories of human needs, talents, or interests from each other. We repeat our assertion, then, that discrete institutions do not exist. What modernity has manufactured is a reality that is not of the character it supposes. Society *seems* to be institutionally divided society and people *seem* to be hierarchically partialized individuals, but neither is a valid description. The authoritative model of both persons and institutions is wrong. But something does exist. There must be something more than illusions or delusions. Let us turn now to what does exist.

3

Institutional Appearances: Three Kinds of Consciousness

Let us be clear on what we have concluded so far. In regard to the house-building industry, we have found that neither the objects produced by the industry for consumption or use nor the activities of either house production or house consumption are a sufficient basis for concluding that such an industry is, in its essential character, economic. But an economic institution, the house-building industry, presumably does exist. People ranging from developers to architects to a host of financial-commercial people to the various electricians, carpenters, truck drivers, and others are engaged in the human enterprise of house building. People as customers, as buyers or renters, order or accept the products. On the one side people are engaged in making money for their survival, and on the other side people are engaged in obtaining shelter, also for their survival. Is this not patently economic? What are the illusions or delusions that are involved?

Let us also be clear that our model of a total person is not a composite or a result of an additive process applied to submodels. In fact, the model of a total person is the overarching model; it does not preclude submodels of people, of people understood as analytically reduced from their humanity to something less. These more fragmentary submodels are various possible infra- or extrahuman pictures, sometimes of a functional and sometimes of a structural kind, each picture having its own specification of needs and/or capabilities. There may or may not be ways to connect various submodels to the encompassing model of a total person. The ways are not known today.

But it is just these submodels that distinguish institutional enterprises. People and institutions both are partialized, and neither total persons nor total societies can be formed by an attempt to put Humpty Dumpty together again. The result of this fragmentation is a widespread, deepening false consciousness, and human effort is misplaced in trying to solve false problems in an illusory or delusory manner. Let us be more specific.

Returning to the example of the house-building industry, what do we find? A central delusion is that such an industry is adequately understood, that is, understood with at least a modicum of validity, as being essentially an economic institution (or subinstitution). This means that people involved therein are centrally concerned with wealth, with the creation, distribution, etc., of wealth, whether as producers or as consumers, not because they generate such an interest personally, subjectively, but because of the nature of the industry, its activities and objects. If institutional distinctions were merely interests generated by people, the nature of an institution could be mixed, muddied, or changed as easily as people changed their perspectives.

Moreover, and this is the second major delusion, institutions are considered suprapersonal. As we said in the very beginning, institutional enterprises are supposedly something greater and more permanent than the people participating therein. They have something of a suprahuman quality. This quality makes an institution something too difficult to change merely by people changing their personal perspectives or interests and makes a society of institutions something more than merely a society of persons living in person-to-person social space.

The house-building industry is but one of numerous examples of institutions termed "economic" essentially because people are working at the creation, the production, of useful objects that they or others want. With the division of labor, then we have—over-simply—producers, houses, and consumers. The houses themselves are understood as meeting or satisfying the partialized, objectified needs of people for shelter—some of the human biological needs if you will. But consumers are *people* understood not as users of such objects for their physiological or biological needs, as one might understand an animal's need for shelter. People are better understood as wanting houses, having interest in houses, valuing houses precisely for the human values implicit or potential in persons using such physical objects as houses. A house to a person is not a value per se.

First of all, houses are not in and of themselves wanted by people. People want them for the experiences of having shelter from the elements, of having warmth instead of cold, of being dry instead of wet, of having a place for pleasurable dining and for sociable and sexual experiences—these are all values, signifying the human meaning of a house. Even the experience of wanting a house for the financial security or wealth it may signify is a value. The "use value" of a house, to use a term borrowed from economists, is precisely the value to people of such an object in terms of its potential for providing desired human experiences.

But in the modern society, the economist's market values have become predominant. There is no possibility of admitting other human values into such a fiscal calculus. In fact, although some economists use the broad term "utilities" while others are concentrating on such aggregate utilities as are associated with the term "welfare," exchange values had already, by the time of the classical economists and Marx himself, driven out use values as an important concept for economists qua economists.

To equate exchange and use values is something modern economists would not do seriously except that in the absence of any independent measures of the latter, economic theorists often do exactly that. They are saved from serious professional criticism because when they do so, they can claim it is merely an incidental assumption or a useful fiction. Today use values are not in the domain of the economist but in that of the politician, plain people, or whoever else wants them, if anyone does.[1]

The economist is blocked from moving beyond the prices of houses to the broader range of use values that houses have for people. Even if a house per se were valued in the sense of a person wanting to possess it, the question would be, Why the desire for possession? The answer would be for security, for future exchange, for its potential increase in monetary value, etc. But the economist has no reasonable way to raise the question of motives beyond prices asked or paid.

We shall stay with economics a bit longer. Even if the economist and the economic institution cannot take directly into account or speak to matters of use values, prices and monetary values do so indirectly for consumers and even more directly for producers. Presumably the economist can, indeed must, speak of money when speaking of the myriad of people and kinds of special and not-so-special but still specialized work involved in building houses. The assumption must be that people work for money, and when this is the case, as we indicated in the previous chapter we have the guideline that an institutional enterprise is economic.

But we have indicated also that such an assumption is faulty. We can indeed find a basis for common categorization of people engaged in house building in regard to their contributions to a defined object, houses. They are engaged in activities that consciously or not, subjectively or not, are directed to the human biological need for shelter. We have, then, the objective criterion that we seek, but what we have is the criterion for categorizing sets of persons as contributing to a *house-building industry*. That such an ''industry'' deserves to be known as ''economic,'' as an ''economic institution'' or a portion of an economic institution, as a part of an ''economy'' is not demonstrated by that conclusion.

If at least all the producers are working for money, is this not a conclusive finding? Is this not an equally objective fact in the sense of applying at least minimally to all the subjective persons engaged in production? No, it is not. It is not because, as we have suggested, people do not work always or necessarily to make money, certainly not exclusively for money, and certainly all people do not work equally exclusively for money.

Suppose we adopted the very broad conception of production that was at the core of Marx's political economy. Whenever human beings engaged in purposeful activity, they were producing, hence engaging in economic activity. Economic activities, then, ranged from the basic matters of producing food, clothing, and shelter through the equally basic matter of producing children and included along the way at the very least the artistic works of Michelangelo and Raphael. The problem, of course, is that all activities and all institutions are then economic with the exception, perhaps, of merely playful (presumably purposeless) ones and, also for Marx, of religion (which he conceived of as being for people's personal pleasure when not used for the political/economic purposes of the dominant class).

A narrower conception of production is possible, but it involves the problems described earlier. If economic activity and economic institutions are those wherein people work for money, the crucial fact is not in the nature of the objects produced or the needs addressed but in the subjective matter of interests on the part of the people participating in the production. Distinguishing institutions and their activities becomes, then, precisely a matter of ascertaining the ordinarily more than single and very subjective motives of the participants in production.

Efforts have been made both by classical economists and by Marx himself to refine the narrow conception even further. Work or labor has been further divided into that which is merely labor in that it does not contribute to capital and so-called productive labor, which does so contribute. Beyond resulting in various services being regarded as nonproductive labor, such a distinction has added little or nothing to the development of a clear means of differentiating basic institutions or human activities.

The first delusion in summary, then, is to suppose that people engaged as either producers or consumers in the house-building industry are there with merely one motive: to make money or to possess a house. It is a delusion to think that while people work or buy they are not *simultaneously* engaging in social relations, in influence relations, in the gamut of human-experiential values, rather than merely in the more narrowly defined wealth-creating or wealth-related affairs of goods and services.

It is a twofold delusion. First, people are deluded when they think their "economic" activity or involvement in "economic institutions" or in "the economy" is so termed and understood as a result of any objective definition of the activity; this is the most subjective of grounds. Second, people are deluded into thinking that even if they develop a single motive or single-minded interest, e.g., making money, it is possible to exercise their faculties in such a manner as to exclude the other facets and the other faculties that are always involved in human activity. If extreme, such a delusion can be an indication of madness. But if widely shared, as it is in a society such as ours, persons can and do operate with these visions and they are confirmed as sane by other persons, although we shall speak shortly of various degrees of consciousness of the falsity of these visions as well as about their increasingly negative consequences.

As a consequence of the double-headed delusion, people slowly but surely have come to regard noneconomic institutions as also economic. Commercial motives have infiltrated into so many spaces that, indeed, developed capitalist society does seem to have become one giant economy. But this "infiltration" is precisely one of people developing economic motives to such an extreme that it *appears* that all institutions deserve to be labeled "economic." Earlier noneconomic features regarded as fundamental and in the nature of things became so diminished that institutional differentiations seem to have disappeared. Not only that, but people have come increasingly to regard their lives as marked by an absence or near absence of the various noneconomic aspects their grandparents knew when not on the job. When on the job, people today tend to believe that the kind of noneconomic aspects of human relations known by earlier generations, prior to the extreme specialization and divisions of labor and life, are not present when indeed they are present.

But let us turn from economic to other institutions. We find that just as the economist is blocked from moving beyond a monetary or price calculus to the broader range of human interests or values, disciplinary specialists of other institutions are similarly halted from inquiring systematically or deeply into human values that are presumably beyond the pale of their particular institution. Culture or art, for example, supposedly being at or toward the opposite pole from purposeful work, that is, being a kind of play, evidences comparably artificial and distorting central concerns as well as boundaries. The reason is the same: institutional thinking. And what we will now say does not lose its validity if the reader prefers to view culture and art as domains of so-called high culture, that is, not as play but as the most serious, unplayful aesthetic pleasures.

Cultural institutions presumably exist for something other than the need of man merely for possession or consumption of mundane objects of utility. If the production of artistic objects were done in the context of commerce, we would have an economic institution (or subinstitution) rather than or at least mixed with a cultural institution. The matter gets terribly sticky if we ask what the difference is between consuming an ordinary "economic" service and consuming a "cultural" service or what the difference is in the utility of economic and artistic objects. Is the nature of an artistic object or performance different from that of the economy, as Engels suggested in the quotation offered earlier?

Historically, many definitions of an aesthetic experience have been offered. We shall not attempt to indicate which we consider best or to offer our own. But we must comment on the nature of aesthetic experiences despite the lack of a definition.

We agree that people have a need for the aesthetic. Just as an animal does, a person has a biological (-physiological-chemical) need to make contrasts, distinguish forms, see and act in perspective, or whatever is the aesthetic process or however it is understood or verbalized. This need encompasses or rests upon the human's animallike abilities, faculties, etc., among which are economic and other distinguishable need categories.

However, at the level of total human beings, the aesthetic becomes incorporated into a human experience, a human value. As such, it merges into and becomes a facet of a more holistic experiential unit. Except at the very extreme, which can be only momentary, the experience is not properly described as an aesthetic one. The aesthetic facet is an integral aspect of a broader spectrum fused from the underlying infrahuman dimensions of all living creatures.

Our approach may be contrasted with traditional conceptions of the world as well as with the traditional disciplinary approaches and models by means of a simple diagram. The traditional, indeed, the modern, conception is set out on the left, and our understanding, termed the ''postmodern'' approach, is on the extreme right. As one moves from left to right in this diagram, one moves from the more analytic, partialized approaches and their key terms to the more holistically human and the terms more compatible with this approach. The cell marked * is empty to signify the dearth of agreed-upon language, practices, and even conscious concern with that vast, encompassing, and uniquely human domain. The conscious and self-conscious human effort to understand and/or to improve human conditions is for the most part carried out, even in the so-called humanities, within the institutional consciousness represented by the left-hand portion of this sketch.

Moving even farther to the left than we have diagramed, that is, moving into various disciplines developed to analyze parts of the world and of living creatures, we would find further subdivision of the input/need categories. The aesthetic could be broken down into studies and theories of perception (physiologically), of the emotions (physically), etc. The innate needs category is often extended to include aesthetic talents as a kind of primal underlying physical and/or mysterious capability of people, entering with conception and developing from infancy. When such talents are regarded more as part of human interests, they may be regarded as being contained by the encompassing category of values. There are different theories stressing sometimes inherited (physical) and sometimes environ-

MODERN	POSTMODERN

Partialized Individuals		TOTAL PERSONS

Objectively real		Subjectively real
Innate needs (institutional values)		Human values
Faculties	Talents	Interests
Inputs/outputs		Participation
Activities	Roles	Practices

Consuming . . . Producing — Performing — Creating . . . Re-creating

Products, Things, Objects Goods, Services		EXPERIENCES, POTENTIALS

Behavior	Personality	Character

INSTITUTIONS		EVERYDAY LIFE	
Professional specializations		Human communities	
Economic	F		
Governmental/political	U		
Educational	N		L
Artistic	C		I
Religious	T	*	V
Scientific	I		I
Social	O		N
Recreational	N		G
Everyday life:	I		
relaxation and	N		
socializing	G		

47

mental (historical) factors, as well as theories of aesthetics that attempt to include both.[2]

Managers hire talent, not people . . . was recently written by the president of a Dallas corporation.[3] In these few words we find distilled the modern wisdom. And in the second part of this sentence we find a theory that implies that talents are subject to social shaping, to educational development. In fact, the writer suggests that job inequalities between women and men are due not to prejudice on the part of male managers but to the unsatisfactory schooling women receive: "And if more men than women have been trained in the talents that are required, then men are going to get the jobs." Our point is not that this person is wrong or right in his judgment about the realities of sexual inequalities in employment. It is rather that even many self-proclaimed progressive people would find his attitude that talents are not fixed at birth a congenial point of view and his pithy comment that "managers hire talent, not people" at least essentially true. Of course *people* are hired, but their personhood is of secondary importance. Some people might add a sorrowful "alas," while others might emphasize that here is the secret of the successful American enterprise, which few other nationalities except perhaps some Scandinavians and the Germans have understood. In any event, we would locate our wise modernist securely on the left side of our diagram even though his institutional reality is not rooted in genetic structure, as it is in some views of sexual/social differences.

We have arranged the diagram to indicate that those who work in the context of the left side are dealing with partialized-person models while those who work on the right side are dealing with total-person models. The total-person concept encompasses the partialized individual. It is the total-person side that is least understood and least developed in modernity. One of the reasons it is least developed is that there is an assumed identity between or direct outgrowth from institutions grounded in innate needs and institutions wherein human beings supposedly express and value as human beings.

In our judgment *everyday life* is the domain that even now encompasses what are thought to be institutional projects satisfying distinguishable human needs but which should be understood as human-value projects wherein people are pursuing and having institutionally cross-cutting or extrainstitutional total experiential moments. We shall elaborate on this encompassing conception of everyday life later. Let us return to the aesthetic now.

There is a widespread belief that at the root of the development of the institutions termed "cultural" (literature, painting, music, dance, sculpture, etc.) is the human need for the aesthetic experience. Whether everyone experiences it is debatable; that some people have a greater need and/or capability for such an experience is less debatable. While in so-called primitive societies the cultural institutions are usually interwoven with the everyday life of the people and are open to all, our modern cultural institutions tend to be exclusive and certainly are specialized. How else to efficiently meet the cultural needs of the elite and/or the mass?

It is precisely such thinking that makes some institutions cultural. Conversely, it is such thinking that blinds us to the aesthetic experiences embedded in and shaping human-experiential moments that we have been educated to automatically regard as nonaesthetic. We feel that some moments are free of any aesthetic aspects because they are symbolized as being other kinds of needs, as belonging to other institutional domains, as pertaining to other kinds of human values than the aesthetic, however "aesthetic" may be defined. Such feelings are real but wrong.

One root error of thinking that aesthetic experiences could be restricted to institutionally defined domains or that aesthetics were not present in all human-experiential moments was this concept of a discrete aesthetic experience. Given the long history of elite societies before our own era of democracy, it was not surprising that the educated among them, as well as the philosophers, based their privileged position as possessors of valuable artworks (as well as more mundane economic valuables and ruling power) on experiences that only the few could have had and valued fully. These experiences supposedly resulted from innate faculties and talents. Talented artisans could also have had such an aesthetic experience, but since their talents were restricted to the aesthetic domain they could merely make and not enjoy as the deservedly rich people of some leisure could do.

Of course such beliefs have not evaporated suddenly with modern democracy—even though those entitled to access to the artistic institutions are more numerous than in early periods of postprimitive societies. People of ''refined taste'' now are a larger set than merely members of the elite, and such taste may even be acquired in schools of fine art today.

Another root error was the (even currently) difficult to dislodge notion that from the activities directly connected to innate aesthetic needs and faculties came objects that embodied the qualities of these partialized needs and faculties, hence the world of objets d'art. We have numerous examples of thinking that in an object, whether a painting, a sculpture, or a building, there is an inherent beauty, due to proportions that are naturally proper or for other reasons. Such qualities *in* and *of objects* activate aesthetic pleasure in the beholder if the person has the appropriate aesthetic faculty. It is not accidental that a major aspect of today's efforts to improve cities is to make them beautiful by constructing beautiful buildings, monuments, and other beautifully built objects.

Why do we fault such thinking? Why do we call it a root error? We do so because it is a misleading statement about a building or any object. As Marx himself at least sometimes insisted, no product is completed until consumed. No object can be understood as containing within it beauty per se. Beauty and the appropriate aesthetic experience are always a matter of a subjective person actively experiencing. The person's personally and subjectively shaped sense of beauty is actually expressed in moments wherein the other aspects of being human are present, however much pervaded by the aesthetic kind of pleasure. The latter is not possible without the underlying biological/physical structures of the person being present, but the human-valuational moment obtains essential qualities of a *human* aesthetic experience from that human's history.

It is not that a person cannot experience as a person a building as beautiful. It is that when a person concentrates such that the aesthetic experience dominates, flooding all other, ever-present aspects of a human experience, this is an extreme and unusual kind of human experience. Not only can people not live either by bread or buildings alone, but neither bread nor buildings can be regarded more than momentarily as humanly satisfying in a unidimensional perspective or experiential frame, whether of economics or aesthetics. It would be better for architects and planners to try to improve the city from a different starting point than the aesthetic as conventionally conceived. And it would be better for social workers and politicians trying to improve the plight of poor city dwellers to start to reduce or eliminate poverty from a different starting point than the economic.

That the notion of aesthetics as residing in the object is difficult to dislodge even today is evidenced in the work of Raymond Williams, the British sociological and literary critic of a neo-Marxist orientation.[4] Williams's argument in summary is this.

In the twentieth century especially, all kinds of theories developed based on the question of how a work of art as an object of consumption affected consumers. A work of art was regarded as an object "in itself as it really is." This belief lent itself to dissecting the work, the object, into its components (even if later the work was reconstituted). This was done not only by the so-called New Critics in literature; it lent itself nicely to Marxist analysis of art objects in terms of base and superstructure. The components of an artwork's production were the real activities of the base. Thus art objects could be treated as more important in terms of their production and less important, i.e., superstructural, in their consumption.

Williams suggests that the contemporary crisis in cultural theory lies precisely in "this view of the work of art as object and the alternative view of art as a practice."[5] He is quite correct in suggesting how in literature—especially in drama—in music, and in many of the performing arts, we have notations requiring interpretation. He has a very difficult time, however, in separating such notations, which do not have "specific material existence," from objects, which do. We agree fully with the following statement: "These notations have to be interpreted in an active way. . . . But indeed this is true over an even wider field. The relationship between the making of a work of art and the reception of a work of art is always

51

active, and subject to conventions, which in themselves are forms of social organization and relationship.''[6] But we disagree when he completes that sentence by saying ''and this is radically different from the production and consumption of an *object*'' (emphasis added). Williams continues in a somewhat contradictory manner relative to objects: ''It is indeed an activity and a practice, and in its accessible forms, although it may in some arts have the character of a material object, it is still only accessible through active perception and interpretation. This makes the case of notation, in arts like drama and literature and music, only a special case of a much wider truth.'' He starts his discussion with the admission that some works of art do consist of objects and are therefore to be understood and treated differently. After the first aforementioned reference to the alternative views of works of art as objects or as practices, Williams goes on to say: ''Of course it is at once objected that the work of art *is* an object: that various works have survived from the past, particular sculptures, particular paintings, particular buildings, and these are objects. This is of course true, but the same way of thinking is applied to works which have no such material existence.'' He goes on trying to distinguish the literary and performing arts from the visual arts in a manner that contradicts his own insights already quoted:

> There is no *Hamlet*, no *Brothers Karamazov*, no *Wuthering Heights*, in the sense that there is a particular great painting. There is no Fifth Symphony, there is no work in the whole area of music and dance and performance, [sic] which is an object in any way comparable to those works in the visual arts which have survived. And yet the habit of treating all such works as objects has persisted because this is a basic theoretical and practical presupposition.

He ends his discussion with the same kind of refusal to understand fixed material objects in the same manner as he does other works of art, when he speaks of the mode of analysis of the latter as contrasted with that of the former: ''This means, of course, that we have no built-in procedure of the kind which is indicated by the fixed character of an object.''[7]

One point, then, is that even such an acute and sensitive commentator as Raymond Williams, whom we will cite again shortly for another demystifying insight, found it impossible to fully shed himself of the fundamental reality and importance of the object itself in at least one major domain of the arts. But the more important point is Williams's recognition that at least for the practice of literary criticism (albeit itself a specialized kind of practice), the objective basis of many of the institutions of art and culture disappears into a totally human-experiential realm of "literary conventions or . . . social relationships."

No matter, then, how art is differentiated from other aspects of human experiences, whether by innate needs, by activities or objects, or even on the basis of valued interests or practices, as are other institutions it is thought to exist as a pure dimension. This premise is constantly reinforced by the exclusive character of the workings of the so-called institutions. Now we are led to another aspect of the delusion concerning the objective existence of institutions.

As a consequence of our double-headed belief that people single-mindedly pursue objectively distinguishable practices, we acknowledge that people are thereby sorted (that is, they sort themselves and each other) into categories, resulting in some kind of separateness even if not the kind supposed. Our question now is whether such activities as those involved in house building or picture painting or dancing or whatever do take place in an everyday-life space, as we suggested. Do they instead take place in a kind of institutional false consciousness, which, however, is real? We are close to answering the question, What exists if discrete institutions do not?

When we first referred to everyday-life space we suggested human experiences take place at that level, that people there are total persons, total social persons in the transinstitutional, interpersonal sense of the word "social." Despite the conventional usage of the term to denote that everyday life is the bit of life left over after other institutional places and spaces, especially the working place and economic institutions, we conceive of everyday life as the total life space of all persons. But we were ambiguous in speaking of the everyday-life space earlier.

We had suggested that people participate in "commonly understood'' experiences as total persons. We qualified this statement, however, to say that people are subject to the particular historical peculiarities of language, etc., that characterize their particular historical group setting. We meant that there is only one all-encompassing everyday-life domain populated by total persons, but that these total persons may regard some other persons as fellows speaking the same language and still others as strangers whose language they assume is human although the meaning is not known to them. Alternatively, these total persons may regard others as aliens, as creatures whose language and experiences probably would not resemble theirs; in any event there is no likelihood of ever finding out. Finally, these total persons may regard themselves as such, as whole persons, or else as specialists whose language and experience can be shared and understood only by fellow specialists or by people with the same institutional membership.

In the following pages we use the terms ''language,'' ''practice,'' and ''human experience'' substantially interchangeably. The term practice is generally defined as human activity that has meaning(s) attached to it, as activity in one or more of its human significances. Lasswell and Kaplan define a practice as ''an act characterized according to the kind of operation and the perspectives in which it is performed.''[8] Language is a communicative act that also has meaning embedded in it. By language we do not mean merely speech and writing; it includes expressive and instrumental bodily movements of all kinds, that is, operations that entail meaning. Human experience, a human-experiential moment or unit, is a synonym for language and practice. In the discussion of institutional specialization and consciousness that follows, we shall refer to the economic institutions although the example can be applied to all institutions.

People in the modern world of work, whether blue collar workers on an assembly line or professional engineers or scientists, are subject to special languages and practices in their everyday working lives. They are embedded in a matrix of communicative interactions that enforce and reinforce the idea that they are experiencing not as total persons but as functional roles. These roles signify that the persons are engaged in an enterprise devoted to the satisfaction of human needs for possession or consumption of goods or services, however more detailed may be the description of the particular enterprise.

Whether we are industrial workers, engineers, architects, or professors of social science, our consciousness is affected by the signs, symbols, and signals that surround us, especially for long periods of our waking hours, that is, in our working hours. We assert, however, that despite everyone's being subjected to such a process, modern man can be roughly sorted into three not tightly bounded categories in regard to institutional shaping of consciousness.

One category includes people whose consciousness is pretty much determined by such specialized and partialized communicative interactional environments. We refer to this category as "institutional consciousness."

A second category includes a few people who are not at all deluded that such institutionally defined experiences conceived in such partialized ways constitute the true meaning of what they are experiencing. The few who reject institutional reality as being a false consciousness may be found amusing and diverting by fellow workers, but they run the risk of being declared at least eccentrics if not troublemakers or even lunatics by those of their fellows who evidence what we termed institutional consciousness. We may term such people the "truly" or "totally conscious."

Finally, in a third category there are people who maintain a kind of double consciousness. They are conscious of the partial and partializing human experiences in which they are engaged as members of institutions and also of the truly and totally human experiences in which they are engaged at the same time in the same place. The latter awareness may be subconscious or barely conscious, intermittent or fully conscious. If fully conscious but mixed with an equally conscious sense of being less than a total person, we have a divided, confused consciousness.

Institutional consciousness we regard as false consciousness, as perhaps *the* modern false consciousness. It is false in the sense that it accepts the fiction that the enterprise is concerned with divided, distinct processes of production and consumption. It accepts the myth that products are desired only or even at all for their own sake, for the sake of their possession or consumption, apart from matters of power, of social relations, and even of wealth that products imply. Moreover, people of such consciousness accept the idea that somehow they are less than total people as they engage in such activities. They often and perhaps increasingly feel that they are violating the nature of economic institutional reality if noneconomic moments of friendship and sociability appear. They may even feel guilty if recreational and educational events occur on the job and in the job. Worst of all, if they begin to regard their direct work activities as entailing such events rather than being solely a serious concentration on the task at hand in the interest of rationality, efficiency, and economy, of higher wages if not higher profits, they may feel properly punished if and when caught. They have violated not merely a human contract to focus subjective interests but also the very nature of the specialized, distinct economic institutional world.

Although people suspect that in the higher levels of economic organization, in the suites atop the skyscraping office towers and even, on a rare occasion, in the scientist's laboratory, people do play politics, this is not quite accepted. It is neither expected nor accepted in the mines or on the assembly lines, and generally politics is thought a kind of human behavior that should be outside serious economic or scientific or cultural operations.[9] It is not possible, however, to understand the human-experiential moments in a factory, office, or research laboratory without interpersonal influence and power, sociability, enlightenment, aesthetics.

Here, then, is Engels' sense of institutions of which we spoke. Politics exists only in the "state institutions"; to make sense of the world one has to posit discrete institutions. Marx as well as Engels often seemed to have a sense that there were two kinds of politics. One "Politics" had a capital "P." This was proper politics, politics of the superstructural institutions of the state. Then there was "politics" with a small "p," a kind of pathetic and impure politics that took place in institutions that would have been better without such politics. Such a sentiment pervades modernity today, embraced as much by conservatives as by those on the left.

But should not people put outside their economic role behavior such distracting if not sordid matters as the pursuit of power and the effort to exercise political influence? Are there not proper times and places for sociability, for enlightenment, for art, for politics? Are not these experiences appropriate for times and places outside the working times and places? Is it not good to delay gratifications?

We asked earlier whether it might not be a mark of maturity to engage in the activities of specialized, discrete institutions. We responded then that such engagement was impossible. The reasons should be clear by now. Institutions in the sense of discrete institutions, specific to one and only one human value or category of values, are impossible to conceive of. But institutions specific to needs of objectified men and women are visualizable, as we have seen. May it not be possible and advisable for people to put outside their ken all the facets of any of their values but for the one at hand? May not human-experiential moments be distilled and sharply focused by concentrating on the task at hand, whether the task be economic or cultural or governmental? In fact, the particular institutional language, customs, rites, robes (if it has special dress) and other distinguishing paraphernalia are useful in such efforts. Can such efforts succeed?

What can and indeed does happen in modernity is that in such human-experiential moments one facet can become predominant while other facets become impoverished. People may put these other facets outside their ken, but it is a fiction to suggest that these facets thereby do not exist. The result of the fiction may be good or bad on balance, but it is our thesis that in modernity it has become increasingly bad for people. When institutions function *as if* discrete human needs exist, but they actually do not, and when institutional members act *as if* human-experiential moments were single-faceted, *as if* a single human value in any human enterprise could be given precedence over all others, it is not surprising that these values or, more properly, the human experiences embodying these values, should become one-sided or distorted.

In an influential essay Herbert Marcuse has suggested that modern people have become one-dimensional.[10] Man is supposedly a commercialized consumer of and in the economy. We do not agree.

People do indeed have a spurious kind of one-dimensional appearance. Those who evidence the aforementioned institutional consciousness are living much of their everyday lives with such a sense of one-dimensionality. But the reality is very different. People may delay gratifications, but in the process they do not *become* partialized economic people.

In an economic enterprise, for example, the person who acts with others strictly in terms of an ensemble of economic roles is unaware of the existing political influence relations there. They exist, however, not only in terms of the functioning of the production process but also in a total political-economic-social sense and, invariably in modernity, hierarchically. Institutional consciousness in such cases serves to foster and maintain a system of domination by total persons of other total persons.

Such institutional consciousness also contributes to the existence of an unrecognized educational process in factories and economic enterprises of all kinds which may be most often characterized as one of educational impoverishment, of diseducation or distorted education. This is the case, while trade union officials, just as corporate managers, take the position that a factory is not at all by its nature an educational entity; a factory is an economic entity. Unions may demand education for the workers, but usually it is intimately connected to jobs or, if not, it takes the form of paid time to pursue education outside the factory.

We may now affirm that maturity consists precisely in seeing through, going behind and beyond, the specificity pretended by institutions, by their creators, by their current leaders, by their influential directors and managers, and, indeed, by many of their rank-and-file members.[11] Maturity consists not of the kind of institutional concentration or delayed gratification mentioned above. Maturity consists of a true consciousness of the multifaceted human moments experienced in all institutional settings and of the potential utilities of products and practices such as houses and police officers who patrol the streets, or at least of homes and of safe, secure passage. We will later on, however, suggest how by opening institutions one may approach such products and practices very differently from the way they are currently approached in a society of such divisions of labor and life.

In other words, maturity is refusing to be filled with the institutional consciousness that there is a human significance in partialized, objectified needs and a distinctness in values and institutional domains.[12] Such maturity can come only after an infancy of undifferentiated moments and a childhood of primitively differentiated moments. Maturity comes with the understanding that institutions are always made up of total people experiencing multifaceted moments as they engage in human-experiential projects.

There may exist a normal process of maturation wherein institutional consciousness develops but then is succeeded by the aforementioned double consciousness, which finally becomes transformed into true consciousness. We do not know whether maturation always or usually follows particular sequences. But we do suggest that such a shift away from the conventional conception of maturity as an adult acceptance of the reality of distinct modern institutions may prove to be useful.

We shall now spend a few moments looking at what we consider to be Karl Marx's double consciousness. In a most cursory, sketchy fashion we shall indicate how, despite coming closer to a true consciousness regarding the nature of persons and institutions than any major thinker during the past two centuries, Marx failed to deeply consider the nature of institutions. His failure still haunts the modern world.

Marx saw far more clearly than most the centrality of the divisions of labor and life in distinguishing human from nonhuman beings and shaping human history. What was remarkable was the fact that despite frequent misinterpretations of the nature of Marx's materialism and despite his own un-Godly posture, he had a teleological sense of an unfolding purpose or fate for man that was one of first generating and then dissolving illusions. Obviously we do not mean illusions in the sense only of phantoms or spirits. We mean, as Marx himself meant, that understandings and appearances of reality were very far from the real reality. And those understandings and appearances shaped and defined the most material, corporeal human actions. They pervaded real persons, persons who were single mind-body units and whose consciousness was even material. Language was for Marx the physically identifiable "practical consciousness."[13] These illusions, then, were part of and helped to define subjectively real people.

What was responsible for such illusions, and what did those illusions include? We find that for Marx nearly everything important to and for people by the time of nineteenth-century capitalism consisted of realities encapsulated in illusions or delusions. The human practices pervading all institutional domains were essentially illusory. What was responsible was the ever-developing, ever finer divisions of labor and life that generated, supported, and reinforced the illusions. And we underline that we are not speaking merely of the so-called superstructural institutions but also and especially of the basic economy and the basic community itself.

We may start, however, with one of the presumably less basic institutions, the state. Marx refers to it as "an illusory communal life" wherein fights for the franchise and the like "are merely illusory forms" in which the real class struggles are being fought.[14] But the community itself has become illusory, a "completely illusory community" in contrast to a "real community." In what regard? In regard to the basic reality of interpersonal association which in a real community breeds real freedom and in an illusory community breeds merely a sense of individual independence, an independence that is actually indifference of people to each other.[15]

Indeed, Marx commented, illusory communities constitute real burdens for people, especially when characterized by a class system, which of course had developed by then. More on class shortly.

On the crucial matter of specialized roles, basic economic roles as well as artistic roles, we turn to the famous passage about future communist compared with then present capitalist society. Here we find Marx's understanding of the process of objectification, which process underlies or forms all the repressive, humanly distorting illusions of which he spoke. It was here Marx suggested that people may become proficient in hunting, fishing, shepherding, or doing criticism "without ever becoming hunter, fisherman, shepherd or critic."[16]

He notes that "so long as activity is not voluntarily, but naturally, divided, man's own deed becomes an *alien power* opposed to him, *which enslaves him* instead of being controlled by him." By a "natural" division of activity, that is, of labor, and institutionally differentiated roles, Marx merely meant that a given person, upon entering a social scene, finds that such divisions and differentiations developed historically, so that the person's reality is something natural, encountered in the natural social environment, rather than something the person has created. And every man's and woman's fate is to become as the others have become and still others are in the process of becoming: "For as soon as the distribution of labour comes into being, each man has a particular, exclusive sphere of activity, which is forced upon him and from which he cannot escape."[17] More: "This fixation of social activity, this consolidation of what we ourselves produce *into an objective power above us,* growing out of our control, thwarting our expectations, bringing to naught our calculations, is one of the chief factors in historical development up till now." (Emphasis added.)

Marx immediately makes clear that he is not a mystic: he is not speaking of the existence of suprapersonal, supernatural forces. Rather, he is speaking of social psychology, or, if you prefer, of a very general ability or talent or even interest of human beings through historical time, until now as then at least, even if not forever. We shall continue to quote at some length lest we be regarded as distorting Marx by selective quotation out of context. A very few paragraphs after making the foregoing comment about an objective power being above us and growing out of our control, he elaborates:

The social power, i.e., the multiplied productive force, which arises through the cooperation of different individuals as it is determined by the division of labour, *appears* to those individuals, since their cooperation is not voluntary but has come about naturally, not as their own united power, but *as an alien force outside of them,* of the origin and goal of which they are ignorant, which they *thus* cannot control, which on the contrary passes through a peculiar series of phases and stages independent of the will and the action of man, nay even being the prime governor of those. (Emphasis added.)[18]

We have, then, a force *appearing* alien. People imagine it as an object, as objectively real. People think they are compelled to act in fixed, differentiated, specialized, and partialized roles because everyone else is doing so; it seems to be the nature of the world. Thus the illusion becomes an understanding of their own and of each other's actual behavior. The actions and the understandings cohere to produce the illusory but actual reality.

Marx offers another illustration that strikes close to home today. With unprecedented high unemployment and high inflation at the same time, we are all increasingly dubious that the economists have any laws about which they may speak. Speaking of the world market, of the so-called laws of supply and demand and of competition, Marx notes that people are "more and more enslaved under a power alien to them." In a parody of Adam Smith's famous invisible hand, Marx notes how trade "rules the whole world through the relation of supply and demand," a relation or set of relations also objectified. Marx put it this way: "As an English economist says [it] hovers over the earth like the fate of the ancients, and with invisible hand allots fortune and misfortune to men, sets up empires and overthrows empires, causes nations to rise and to disappear."[19]

Does Marx really believe that the illusory reality of the division of labor and its specialized, institutionally distinct roles governs people? He sometimes speaks as if he does, but a careful reading suggests that he understands full well that people govern people; people participate in governing and in being governed always in reference to others and simultaneously to themselves.

Marx speaks of the illusory community, of how the social relationships within the division of labor and the class all take on or achieve "an independent existence." What precisely is the nature of this independent existence? Is it, as class for Marx is often supposed to be, a suprapersonal, collectivity-level construct? Does a person encounter in reality such suprapersonal entities as classes or communities of classes or such entities as complexes of specialized institutional roles, with their supra- or subpersonal interrelations? In fact, Marx explains that he means none of these things but that *people believe* all of them and behave accordingly. These beliefs have vast practical, personal, and interpersonal consequences because they infuse and shape not only particular actions or practices of people but their total personalities.

Let us start with Marx on the supposedly independent existence of class.

> The separate individuals form a class only insofar as they have to carry on a common battle against another class; otherwise they are on hostile terms with each other as competitors. On the other hand, the *class* in its turn *achieves an independent existence* over against the individuals, so that the latter find their conditions of existence predestined, and hence have their position in life and their personal development assigned to them by their class, become subsumed under it. *This is the same phenomenon as the subjection of the separate individuals to the division of labor. . . .* This subsuming of individuals under the class brings with it their subjection to all kinds of ideas, etc. (Emphasis added.)[20]

Several important points need be noted. First, a class consists only of individuals,* sometimes in hostile competition but at other times united against other classes and, as Marx notes elsewhere, often or even basically indifferent to each other as persons in the modern world of divided, specialized roles. Second, notice how any given person finds himself or herself confronting people already playing the specialized roles in the division of labor. Thus, a class of persons subjects any given person to the kinds of ideas, personal development, and roles regarded as appropriate or fated for members of that class. And it is as much an innocent as a conspiratorial subjection.

It is precisely the same with the supposedly independent social relations within the division of labor:

> . . . in the course of historical evolution and precisely through the inevitable fact that within the division of labour social relationships take on an independent existence, there appears a division within the life of each individual, insofar as it is personal and insofar as it is determined by some branch of labour and the conditions pertaining to it. (*We do not mean it to*

---

*Although Marx also feels that people are partialized, he employs the word "individual" in a general sense unlike our use of "individual" to mean a partialized person.

be understood from this that, for example, the rentier, the capitalist, etc.
cease to be persons; but their personality is conditioned and determined
by quite definite class relationships.) (Emphasis added.)[21]

We find, then, that for Marx modern reality was filled with illusions about a seemingly independent existence of classes and about social relations among specialized roles just as much as about commodity relations (commodity fetishism). Class existence was real but it was not of objects. It was of persons and their interpersonal relations. Because of these illusions, persons treated each other as something other or less than total persons; as commodities, as roles, as classes, or as communities of independent individuals. But, as Marx said of people identified by their economic, hence class, function (as rentiers, capitalists, etc.), such people did not cease to be people. We admit that total persons may have convoluted, crippled, or just plain nasty personalities. We not only admit but even emphasize that total persons may live and experience in a world of distorted, illusory, or even delusory appearances. Yet we do not believe nor did Marx think that these illusory practices merely appeared without rhyme or reason. What was Marx's sense of the origins of the modern hallucinations, the modern fetishism?

In fact, just as the "productions of the human brain appear as independent beings endowed with life" in "the mist-enveloped regions of the religious world," fetishism or the similar feeling that products of human hands are living beings "is therefore inseparable from the production of commodities."[22] Commodity production and all its associated illusions came from the introduction of ever more specialized machines into an increasingly divided division of labor. More efficiency meant more capital accumulation, and the rhythms and rulers of feudalism gave way to those of the modern capitalist era.

What passed away? The feudal ties of "personal dependence, of distinctions of blood, education, etc. are in fact exploded, ripped up."[23] Handicraft work, which was "the regulating principle of social production," is swept away and with it manufacturing as "an economic work of art."[24] Not only are the skill and virtuosity of handicraft work virtually eliminated, but the science that results in machine design "does not exist in the worker's consciousness." Instead it "acts upon him through the machine as an alien power as the power of the machine itself."[25]

What passed away, then, was the possibility for people to participate with a sense of personal potency or of place in an understandable network of human dependency and interdependency relations. What also passed away was the possibility of personally contributing one's skills—one's semiartistic, handicraft, or artisanal skills—in production. Finally, what passed away was any sense of the overall design of the division of labor, and people felt themselves to be no more than cogs in an "invisible machine," to use a phrase of Lewis Mumford. It was a machine which few understood but in which all felt compelled to work.

And in future? People will heal the split that has for so long served as a fundamental fault line underlying all divisions of labor. All time will become "free time," time wherein people are not compelled to work and to obey. Processes and moments of production or play, work or leisure, will become single processes and single moments. Thus people will become different; they will, for example, find their fulfillment in working voluntarily rather than being crippled by repetitious, trivial work and being "thus reduced to a fragment of a man."[26] Science will become something other than the development of machines that are programmed automatons and people who are merely assistants to automatons. Workers, that is, all persons who work, will engage in "practice, experimental science, materially creative and objectifying science, as regards the human being who has become, in whose head exists the accumulated knowledge of society."[27]

Persons for Marx are subject to history. They make objects and can do so in future if they can participate as total persons in a noncrippling, nondividing, nonpartializing human fabric. Science will serve people by allowing all men, all women, all workers to participate in science as scientific workers creating the material objects people desire for their life experience. Any thought that Marx himself was trapped into feeling he was living in a world filled by really objective objectifications, substantially material objects with a significance apart from the purposeful human relations that give them meaning, must disintegrate before such sentiments as these:

> When we consider bourgeois society in the long view as a whole, then the final result of the process of social production always appears as the society itself, i.e., the human being itself in its social relations. Everything that has a fixed form, such as the product etc., appears as merely a moment, a vanishing moment, in this movement. The direct production process itself here appears only as a movement. The conditions and objectifications of the process are themselves equally moments of it, and its only subjects are the individuals, but individuals in mutual relationships, which they equally reproduce and produce anew. The constant process of their own movement, in which they renew themselves even as they renew the world of wealth they create. . .[28]

The division of labor, with its fixed, specialized roles, will give way, and fragments of a person will be replaced "by the fully developed individual, fit for a variety of labours, ready to face any change of production, and to whom the different social functions he performs, are but so many modes of giving free scope to his natural and acquired powers."[29] Well, then, in the light of such a deep sense of the devastating illusions surrounding and being shaped by persons performing in and contributing further to the fundamental divisions of labor and life, which divisions he was sure could be overcome in future and would become historically outdated figments of imagination and practices, why do we say that Marx had a kind of double consciousness? It is because he took for granted the reality of institutional divisions without taking the final step of deeply considering and demystifying the basic institutional categories themselves.

In what we have presented from Marx so far, we started with the comparatively early Marx, in his late twenties, of *The German Ideology* (with Engels); continued with the middle-aged Marx of *The Grundrisse*; and ended with the somewhat older Marx of *Capital, Volume I*. This was a span of about twenty years, each work coming some ten years after its predecessor. There was, indeed, a great consistency therein. And there was present an overarching understanding of how the divisions of labor and life had cut up and crippled, paralyzed and partialized people into fragments of their potential selves.

At the same time, however, Marx adhered uncritically to a model of man and of society, both historically forged, which posited a person of multiple categorical needs and corresponding need-satisfying institutions—however unnecessarily fragmenting the results. When we say "uncritically," we mean that he did not think deeply about the meaning of the basic categorical divisions of intrapersonal needs and need-satisfying productive institutions. He did not really question the meaning of "social," "political," "artistic," "religious," and "economic" or "productive" in their more limited sense. His own sense of their apparent reality, however infused by illusions, led him to propose a model and a method for further understanding which has resulted in confusion. In fact, it has confounded many of his other demystifying insights. And it contributed greatly to his own insufficient remedy for solving the problem of the divisions of labor and life, namely, class war and revolution.

Although starting with the conception of production writ large, Marx in the very first book mentioned above, *The German Ideology*, slipped from the broad to the narrow meaning of "production," seemingly without awareness. Production initially covered the gamut of things people produce for use, whatever the domain. Interwoven with material production was the production "of ideas, of conceptions, of consciousness." Mental production was "expressed in the language of politics, laws, morality, religion, metaphysics, etc."[30] Men and women produced children and reproduced themselves. But very early Marx began to speak of the mode of production in conventionally narrow economic terms. The social mode, the social stage, the social structure is somehow distinct from the economic: "By social we understand the cooperation of several individuals. . . . It follows from this that a certain mode of production, *or industrial stage*, is always combined with a certain mode of cooperation, *or social stage*, and this mode of co-operation is itself a 'productive force.' " (Emphasis added.)[31] So, too, does the state emerge, and the beginning of the base-superstructure duality theory: "The social structure and the State are continually evolving out of the life-process of definite individuals . . . i.e., as they operate, produce materially, and hence as they work under definite material limits, presuppositions and conditions independent of their will."[32] And even within the limited divisions of labor in the feudal epoch, Marx understood relations as divisible into at least three parts: productive, i.e., economic; social; and political.[33]

Marx assigned the all-embracing term "civil society" to the life process of which he spoke. Civil society is the "form of intercourse determined by the existing productive forces."[34] It "embraces the whole material intercourse of individuals within a definite stage of the development of productive forces." Civil society "embraces the whole commercial and industrial life of a given stage and, insofar, transcends the State and the nation."[35] In fact, from the civil society comes the state, not as a once-and-for-all entity on its own but as a "continually evolving," functionally necessary "side." Continuing the foregoing sentence: "Civil Society. . . . transcends the State and the nation, though . . . it must assert itself in its foreign relations as nationality, and inwardly must organize itself as State."

The model Marx developed is stated succinctly in the following paragraph:

This conception of history depends on our ability to expound the real process of production, starting out from the material *production of life itself,* and to comprehend the form of intercourse *connected* with this and created by *this mode of production* (i.e., *civil society* in its various stages), as the basis of all history; and to show *it* in action *as State,* to explain all the different theoretical products and forms of consciousness, religion, philosophy, ethics, etc. etc. and trace their origins and growth from that basis; by which means, of course, the whole thing can be depicted *in its totality* (and therefore, too, the reciprocal action *of these various sides* on one another). (All emphasis added.)[36]

We have, then, a state that is part of the "idealistic superstructure" on the one hand and part of the basic civil society on the other. Together, and with such other "sides" as the religious, the philosophic, etc., we have a totality, a whole, wherein these sides reciprocally act on each other. There are shades of logical positivism and the "bourgeois" scientific approach in Marx's comment that "empirical observations must in each separate instance bring out empirically, and without any mystification and speculation, the connection of the social and political structure with production."[37]

Is the state the same thing as the political structure? Is the social structure that evolves out of the civil society a feature, a facet, a side of the industrial-commercial mode of production, of the economic structure? Can the social and economic structures interact, or are they always present together, part of a single inseparable and indivisible texture? Are the connections and interconnections those between a dominating or influencing base and a dominated or influenced superstructure? All such questions flow from the quite unclear referents of Marx's terms: the social, the political, the religious, the commercial-industrial mode of production, etc.

We do not disagree with Marx's motion that a society can be understood as a totality, as a "rich totality of many determinations."[38] It is indeed a "concentration of many determinations, hence, [a] unity of the diverse," this "concrete, living whole."[39] But we do suggest that Marx failed to deeply consider the nature of seemingly easily distinguishable institutions; he instead considered them his undefined primitives, conceptions so obvious they really did not need further defining. This failure led Marx into ambiguities and into a belief that revolution was the necessary and sufficient way for people to obtain a postcapitalist liberation.

It has been said almost ad nauseum that Marx was betrayed or his memory besmirched, if not by Lenin then certainly by Stalin. Instead of a single class taking power, taking over the state and directing the economy, a small elite of bureaucrats and politicians have ruled the working class, albeit in its name. We agree, but our point is different. It is that modernity has witnessed an extreme development of specialized, usually hierarchical institutions whose elites justify their continued domination by pointing to the necessary functioning of their own institutions. Each institution is presumed naturally distinct from the others, even if all touch, are connected to, or act upon each other. Even if the revolution had not been betrayed, then, Marx's own failure to think as deeply about the fundamental institutional

69

categories as he had about so many other illusory objectifications was reason enough for him to miss the possibility of embedding the divisions of labor and life in a more "real community" matrix by a process other than through a revolutionary dictatorship of the proletariat.

It is also sufficient to explain why, quite apart from power-maintaining motives, there is little or no movement in the Soviet Union or in most of its satellite states (Yugoslavia is not a Soviet satellite) by proclaimed Marxists, any more than in the adversary United States of America, to fundamentally alter a finer set of divisions of labor and life than even Marx could have imagined.

With basic institutions untouched, who can really argue against the single party's role of coordinating and, hence, controlling them in the general interest. Such a rationale may increasingly serve the de facto single-party conditions in noncommunist countries where governments of national emergency (or whatever a ruling coalition is called) are set up for coordinating and harmonizing discrete institutions to prevent otherwise apparently unavoidable breakdown or paralysis in modern complex systems.

In fact, a situation is developing in the noncommunist world which is threatening to strip multiple-party systems of the significance they had once upon a time, and for the same reason. Several parties may still exist, some always in the minority or even with majority-minority rotation, but basic policy making is entrusted to various committees of national or international character. With the appropriate systems analysis expertise to provide for interinstitutional coordination, deemed increasingly imperative, hierarchical reorganization may occur without either the guidance of a communist party or any basic tampering with archaic institutional distinctions.

Although, as we have shown, Marx had no illusions about the suprapersonal character of institutions, his failure to more carefully examine basic institutional divisions in terms of their presumably distinct nature contributed as well to the interrelatedness, indeed, the totality, of class-specialized roles. The maintenance of illusions about and the objectification of a seemingly complex institutional reality have helped to defuse potential revolt of the rich as well as the poor. At the same time it must be said that Marx was more insightful and of less false consciousness than untold numbers of his devotees and followers as well as vast numbers of anti-Marxist critics. The generations following Marx have been subjected to additional years of mythology about the society, the institutions, and the people in and of both.

In the next chapter we continue to consider how institutional consciousness operates as a major feature of everyone's everyday life even if some persons manage to maintain a double consciousness or a few even have a true consciousness.

4

Institutional Realities and Everyday Life

We started to address but have not yet definitively answered the question of what exists if discrete institutions do not. Nor have we directly spoken to the second delusion regarding institutional reality referred to in the previous chapter, that institutions are suprapersonal. We shall speak to the matter of institutional suprapersonal status in the course of briefly describing some aspects of recent American everyday-life reality and the kinds of institutional realities embedded therein. We shall start with the period of the late sixties, when the young revolted against the oppressiveness felt to be constituted by their parents' institutional consciousness and their own future of partialized and subhuman, institutionally specialized roles.

We sympathetically understood but rejected much of that so-called countercultural response to modernity. We were sympathetic because it was obvious that numbers of young and not so young people were shedding or had already shed the pervasive kind of humanly distorting institutional consciousness that their parents had developed in the United States by then. It was not at all an accident that this kind of movement developed first in the most densely and deeply institutionalized modern nation-state and then spread to other developed urban-industrial countries.

The sixties was generally a period when important aspects of institutional consciousness gave way, at least temporarily, before the various movements of young people, students, blacks, and those opposed to the American war in Vietnam. Students, for example, began to understand that their universities had political influence and power structures connected to those of the governments of the larger society. Moreover, these so-called educational institutions began to be appreciated not only for their intimate connections with the larger economic as well as the political system but also as unitary economic-political subsystems themselves.

Blacks most active in the civil rights movement began to appreciate that the seemingly suprapersonal, suprahuman, majestic governments—of law, not of man—actually reduced to the power capable of being marshaled by police officers. A vague, amorphous, but heavy "system," once known in the black everyday-life ghettos by means of the diverse lowly representatives of an anonymous personage termed "The Man" or "whitey," suddenly was identified at the personal level. Suddenly it was understood that the system was held together only by institutionally identified persons in uniform. Black militants shouted the epithets "pig" and "honkey" at institutionally conscious police officers, hoping to provoke them into recognizing their own personhood and therefore their responsibility to personally decide the morality of upholding law and order when it was unjust.

As in any time of revolution or near revolution, that is, at a time of stress for and challenge to the people dominant in the various institutional compartments of a society, much of the mythology associated with these institutions evaporated. It was dissolved by such simple and basic facts as that if and when everyday-life compliance with the authorities diminished, law and order would be maintained by the armed force of police and military personnel still subject to the commands or still loyal to the existing persons in power and/or to their suprapersonal symbols.

But as the youthful cultural revolution developed into the counter-culture, it began to counterpose one myth to the other. The counter-culture was a value orientation as one-sided and untrue as that of the larger society. In fact it was the polar opposite. The larger society's primary values seemed to be private wealth and class power. The opposite and truly human values, it seemed to youthful leaders, were modest incomes and an egalitarian abolition of power. This was to be a radical abolition; not only was government as an institution to be ended but also power and influence were to be avoided in every human relationship. Power was to be replaced by love. It would be neither private nor public; it would be a free good available to everyone in the human collectivities and subcollectivities.

"Make love, not war" was not only an anti-Vietnam War slogan. The slogan expressed the belief that it was possible and desirable to base human relations on such human needs as respect and affection and to entirely eliminate influence, that is, politics generally as well as leadership specifically, from human affairs. Freud's apparent insistence that social-sexual inhibitions are the price of civilization made him ineligible for the role of counterculture prophet. Instead, a variety of native, naïve spokesmen, such as Jerry Rubin and Ken Kesey, were put in the pantheon along with such ultrasophisticated intellectuals as Herbert Marcuse. The latter's glimpse of a liberated society in future was misinterpreted as a call for the end to all repression rather than an end to surplus repression.

In any event, the effort to build counterculture organizations without the exercise of influence and power was an exercise in futility. To be sure, the dominant belief that processes and constituent moments were purely political, purely of influence or power, or purely economic, was and is wrong; but to believe that human-experiential moments can be freed from all facets of interpersonal influence is equally wrong.[1]

We repeat that the countercultural urge to create conditions oppo-site to those they found to be unnecessarily *and increasingly* distort-ing and oppressive to human beings was doomed to failure. It was doomed because the alternative was flawed at its base. The specialized institution of a suprapersonality was to have been replaced by a kind of noninstitutional, nonorganized organization of persons whose own personalities would be flattened by efforts to rid the self of any egoism or by means of the person-shattering, dreamlike creation of illusions through drug taking. The contradiction proved fatal when even loving leadership was proscribed as being subversive of the "only love–no leadership" theme.

The counterculture was also doomed because the balance of power favored the so-called establishment. The crucial weight of power in that balance came from the so-called oppressed—the middle-, lower-middle-, and especially working-class people in whom disheveled clothing, long and unkempt hair, and drugs struck terror. The terror was real; it was a terror of disorder, of breakdown, of anarchy. Better the constriction of institutions than an orgy of irresponsible play making without the decision making that the older generation knew in its bones was a necessary aspect of civilization.

This discussion of the tumultuous movements and countermovements of the late sixties and early seventies gives us an opportunity to speak about the matter of personal and group responsibility in an institutional world. In a modern urban-industrial society of extreme divisions of labor and life, responsibility withers away as effectively as do self-consciously total persons.

It became evident in the civil rights movement that serious and sincere people representing high as well as medium and low strata in the hierarchies of institutions denied having any power or capability to help redress unjust and still occurring injuries to the human rights of black citizens. They proclaimed, still sincerely, no personal or institutional responsibility for these injuries. Similarly, research scientists, engineers, and major corporations of all kinds proclaimed no responsibility for the Vietnam War, a war presumably within the domain of authority of the government and politicians.

In a world of seemingly discrete institutions, it followed that government was the only institution deemed capable of correcting some of the racist injustices and of stopping or prosecuting that war. Because institutions were concentrated on parts of people, on objective needs that were discrete, and were not concerned directly or even indirectly with whole persons and sets of persons in human relationships, the institutionally conscious person could with good conscience claim no or at most very little responsibility for effects on people not within the acknowledged institutional domain or for effects unintended or incidental to the legitimate specialized mission of the institution.

Thus, who today would accept responsibility for the unfortunate, *incidental* consequence that the ever finer divisions of life, produced by ever more refined institutional divisions, result in a social fabric increasingly characterized by widespread personal and interpersonal pathology? Who can be held accountable for nuclear rather than extended families, for social isolation and privatization, and for alienation not only from work but from all the decisions that affect people's immediate living situations? Why should a nuclear physicist working in theoretical science on very abstruse, very professional matters accept any responsibility because the work may be converted by others to evil purposes? Is it the fault of a police department that when their members are very proficient in their professional work the result may be increased racial injustice?

If police officers are instructed to try to prevent crime rather than merely to try to apprehend the criminal after the event, seemingly a progressive effort, they may be told to be alert for suspicious, meaning extraordinary, situations indicating an increased probability of a crime being committed. Given that their professional/technical institutional responsibility is limited to preventing crime and preserving law and order, they would be foolish or incompetent not to investigate the extraordinary appearance of black faces appearing at night in an all-white neighborhood in a de facto racially segregated society. For the one it is good police work, but for the other it is racial harassment.

It is useful in this context to emphasize how human projects termed "institutions" could have been constructed such that total persons and whole groups of total persons would have simply disappeared from the view of an institution's membership. To repeat, the method of making institutions discrete is to assign symbols to various objects

76

and activities and thereafter regard them as economic *or* cultural *or* social *or* political *or*. . . . It has proved useful, for example, to various people, groups, and classes to sustain the myth that work in an ensemble of activities termed an "industry" (work, that is, that produces income) is nothing more than work, only work, or primarily work.

The way this myth is sustained is to treat patently noneconomic features of work practices which are inescapably there as nonexistent, as incidental and trivial, or as *really economic* relations. Thus, an economist studies the production process and the relations of people as they engage in production while leaving to the sociologist, to the industrial sociologist in fact, the study of what the economist conceptualizes as separable: the partialized social relations, the so-called social system of the factory. Industrial or political sociologists or an occasional political scientist have the right to study the factory in its partialized aspects as a political power system or subsystem, although the political scientist is better off sticking to the study of government and of manifestly political institutions, such as political parties.[2] Such specialization in the so-called social sciences does nothing but reinforce the myth of the reality of discrete institutions.

It is not only the police, then, who believe in the independent reality of a partialized institutional concern. Contrary to much expert opinion, the police are quite typical in how they handle the matter of their human responsibilities.

The police conceive of the breakdown of morality, the church, and the family as related to, as causes of, the breakdown of law and order. They may even have a theory that it is pornographic literature and/or drugs that are basic causes of the first set of breakdowns. But the preservation or restoration of law and order is what is their institutional concern.

The police are not charged with repairing or doing anything about even the fundamental cornerstones of law and order that they believe are crumbling. They are not responsible for politics, or for industrial production, and certainly not for art and aesthetics. In such a belief they resemble educators (or whoever from whatever specialized institution) who understand their professional setting as being ideally if not actually entirely free of commercialism, of politics, and of playing—except if the playing is an educational form or is a noneducational moment of relaxation.

For educators there are people not engaged in education, while those who are so engaged become students and something less than total people. For the police there are also invisible people outside the domain of law and order; for example, a research scientist when working in the laboratory (and presumably out of everyday life) is not usually thought of as contributing to or disturbing law and order.

The fiction of discrete institutions, making people partial or even invisible, is maintained by the learned and the illiterate, the high and mighty and the lowly. One reason it may get such contributions is that the consequent escape from responsibilities is something to which many people have grown accustomed. And the escape is not only from a personal responsibility; it extends even to the institution with which a person may identify, whose officials can manage to either shift the responsibility to other institutions or claim that no single institution is largely responsible because the problem is supra- or sub- or transinstitutional in character. During the days of the civil rights movement in the United States, just as today, it was as difficult to find an institution whose leadership admitted major responsibility for the maintenance of segregated patterns and practices as it was to find in post-Nazi Germany any institutional leaders acknowledging any responsibility for the death camps there.

Was it and is it true, or not, as many in the counterculture asserted, just as Marx had more than a century earlier, that a particular kind of one-dimensionality had developed within most if not all of the modern economic institutions? Specifically, was the counterculture correct in asserting that work in the most modern, most automated factories had eliminated the craftsmanship and thus the aesthetic facet? In modern technology's division of jobs into small, often routine and mechanical tasks, is it not true that even if social relations are present, artisanship and art have long since gone from nearly all such industrial work?

This is not merely a countercultural or radical left claim. Many conservatives, liberals, and apolitical people of institutional as well as double consciousness believe it, some happily or with a sense of propriety and others deploring it. The latter would like to introduce at least some reforms in the direction of making the working place and thus work more of an aesthetic experience. Doing this may, of course, take the form of making the decor a bit more "artistic," with pictures on the walls and sculptures in the halls.

Let us approach the matter in this way. Earlier we commented that some people may deny that the aesthetic experience is universal, while fewer will contest the claim that the ability to experience aesthetically is unequally distributed. Our own position is this. The so-called aesthetic experience is indeed a universal capability of human beings. However, as we suggested above, it is not a distinguishable, discrete experience except at the limits. Consequently, it is misleading to refer to an aesthetic experience as such. People may differ in their innate abilities or talents to perform or to appreciate particular forms of artistic expression. It is wrong, however, to assert that any one person has a greater ability to experience aesthetically than another person.

Every person is able to experience almost purely aesthetic moments, that is, moments when all other facets of human experience have been overwhelmed or fused into the pure or predominant state of being that can be appropriately termed aesthetic. The inescapable individuality of people makes it nonsense to differentiate among such extreme moments by degrees of more or less. Moreover and more to the point, all human-experiential moments that are not purely aesthetic include aesthetic facets. This is the case in all human practices.

They include, of course, but extend beyond the so-called cultural, or artistic, and literary practices. In modernity these are the institutionally shaped and defined expressions of performing or forming and appreciating (overlapping, interpenetrated moments of production and consumption, to continue to use the language of economics). To such particularized and humanly shaped modes of expression are attached the technical/professional standards that do come from institutions, that is, from people of and representing the expertise in the institution. It is also precisely when such standards become defined as cultural or artistic for the entire society that various institutionally shaped (technical) kinds and degrees of proficiency substitute for a simple two- or three-category proficiency differentiation, all categories being within the reach of all human beings.

Although he does not explicitly take our position, Raymond Williams evidences something of our spirit when he denies that there are "relations" between art or literature and society:

> The literature is there from the beginning as a practice in the society. Indeed until it and all other practices are present, the society cannot be seen as fully formed. . . . We cannot separate literature and art from other kinds of social practice, in such a way as to make them subject to quite special and distinct laws. They may have quite specific features as practices, but they cannot be separated from the general social process. . . . Without the sleight-of-hand of calling Literature only that which we have already selected as embodying certain meanings and values at a certain scale of intensity, we are bound to recognize that the act of writing, the practices of discourse in writing and speech, the making of novels and poems and plays and theories, all this activity takes place in all areas of the culture.[3]

We believe that even the machinelike, repetitive, monotonous operations of workers on an assembly line contain an aesthetic facet. These human-experiential moments are indeed deadly dull or worse. The operations are likely to break the body and spirit of the workers; they are likely to enfeeble them mentally, physically, and/or emotionally. They are like bad paintings, only worse. At least one can shut one's eyes or walk away from an unpleasant painting.

In other words, modern everyday factory experiences are human but crippling to total persons in a variety of regards. They are human-experiential moments wherein the aesthetic facets are sometimes so horribly ugly that they are driven below the level of consciousness, of any kind of consciousness. But they are there, there in all of their ugliness, torment, or sameness. At least, occasionally in some working places men and women of great spirit are found who manage to make the ordinary ugly or tawdry moments ones of great beauty. They have somehow developed a true consciousness. There are even people of double consciousness whose sense of the totality of persons and the multifaceted nature of experiences permits them periodically somehow to bring art and aesthetics into their routine work in a positive fashion.

With industrialization and its mechanization of production, most factory work, as most office work today, is not any longer "still half artistic, half end-in-itself."[4] The skill we associated with artisanship in earlier times has disappeared. It has not been replaced in many of the succeeding modes of industrial/commercial enterprises. But again, this does not mean that the inescapable aesthetic facet of such experiences has disappeared; it has become tawdry or has some other, even more negative qualities. And we do not mean to suggest by the previous paragraph that we think the situation is remediable merely if people rise heroically above their immediate environments and with a true consciousness begin to be satisfied by or even appreciate the beautiful aspects of their often physically, socially, and personally grotesque and maiming circumstances.

The Bauhaus school of design, architecture, and the arts in Germany during the twenties—which included such people as Gropius, Mies Van der Rohe, and Breuer as well as Le Corbusier in both architecture and urban planning—proceeded precisely along the line of trying to improve modern urban-industrial life by improving the beauty of the objects and environments surrounding people. These artists' profound mistake was not to start with people, with total people in their total environments, but to proceed dimension-ally. They recognized as one dimension the major mechanical inno-vations the industrial revolution had brought into the factories and cities. They accepted this dimension as reality and as pretty much the fundamental fabric of the economic and social institutional milieus of their time.

Their task, as experts in beauty, was to make the objects of machine production beautiful by means of artistic designs. They aimed to make the factories and buildings, even housing for workers, beautiful and rational: uncluttered, clean, functional, and efficient, like modern industry. With Le Corbusier the effort to improve life through correct aesthetics led not only to beautiful buildings but also to a system of rational organization of cities based on the machinelike principle that each part is in its place and all parts function in coordinated, smooth movements. Thus, zoning cities into their properly divided areas was the counterpart of neatly divided institutional domains and would presumably produce the city beautiful and good.

But the starting point was wrong, as was the subsequent movement. The Bauhaus designs did not start with people, and they moved along the wrong path in trying to improve the aesthetic dimension. They tried to improve it with technically more beautiful designs and constructions and by extending the aesthetic domain into and around the economic. Artistic institutions of furniture design, of design of all kinds of products, even of factories and machines themselves, as of cities, would be avant garde and would lead the high, fine arts above and beyond lower matters of commerce and money to make the new industrial-artistic society.

The plight of people, of managers as well as workers, of artists and architects, of housewives, of pedestrians, of commuters was understood first and foremost through the eyes of the designer as artist, through machinemade *oeuvres d'art*. Ordinary workers and ordinary consumers would have life improved by this dose of special aesthetics administered by these experts in aesthetics. Despite good intentions, they were bound to fail—although many of them were great financial successes. They were bound to fail because like so many people today, they thought they could solve transinstitutional human problems by working essentially in and on institutionally specialized definitions of the problems without making any major transformations in those definitions. Although sometimes accused of being radicals, they were fundamentally conservatives, as later history demonstrated.

We spoke a while ago of moments that were nearly purely aesthetic. Moments wherein one facet—aesthetic, economic, political, or whatever—is predominant represent the outer limits of extreme subjectivity of man as subjective subject. These are moments that, like some very elementary atomic particles, have but the briefest life span; they are transitory, and for good reason. If the human-experiential moment becomes so one-sided and distorted by being too much of a particular facet for too long, then minimally adequate human activities become impossible.

The converse is also true. If moments are so free of a necessary aspect or if one or another facet constantly squeezes out that aspect, it will prove difficult, if not impossible, to live and experience humanly. So it is with people thrown into solitary confinement in prisons or working in factories, in mines, or under other conditions so brutalized that the aesthetic or other aspect has become impossible to experience. The absence of such a facet is often also transitory because no matter their situation—imprisonment, slavery, or exploitative working conditions—human beings have an immense capability of holding on to their humanity. People often hold on to their ability to live human-experiential moments that include at least the minimum of the necessary facets despite incredibly difficult conditions. Cavemen had their wall paintings, and prisoners have found great beauty in simple stones.

By using the foregoing phrases "necessary aspect" and "necessary facets" have we opened Pandora's box and admitted that man has a set of necessary, therefore basic, and, by implication, also a set of unnecessary or less basic aspects? To the contrary. What we have done is to underline that what generations of people have thought of as needs of persons, of persons objectified as animallike or as social beings, are indeed characteristics integral to all persons. They constitute, as such, "necessary" but equally insufficient and, therefore, equally basic characteristics.

To repeat because the point deserves repetition, all such historically familiar categories of human needs (aesthetic, economic, spiritual, and the like) are necessary ingredients of valuable human experiences. These human-experiential moments may be ordered or ranked in terms of preferred hierarchies of values only subjectively, on the basis of personal moralities or tastes. People may assert, as many people often do, that their preferred ranking is better than others' (for others as well as for the self), but they cannot do so on the basis that theirs represents a natural ordering of needs from the most to the least important, that is, on the basis of a kind of valuefree, scientific objectivity. There may be disagreement over what needs are necessary ingredients of human-experiential moments or how such ''needs'' may be stated. But they cannot be considered either as being discrete or as having differential importance according to the nature of a person when a person is engaged in a human practice.

In any event, our point here is that every human-experiential moment, including ones of working on assembly lines or in scientific research laboratories, must be understood as having an aesthetic quality, whatever its form or condition. There is, indeed, little space left for an artisan's creativity in the modern industrial or commercial enterprise, but this is not because modern society has somehow eliminated the artistic, the aesthetic, from the economic institutional domains and reserved it for presumably more appropriate cultural, artistic, aesthetic institutional domains. Artisanal or artistic creativity and insipid routine are both regions of a given aesthetic dimension.

It might be useful to briefly consider a phenomenological approach to art and the aesthetic. This approach has it that phenomena are understood—or, better, described—as a person ''lives in the midst-of-the-world, as he experiences himself and the world, keenly and acutely, before any kind of reflection whatsoever takes place.''[5] From a phenomenological approach to the art of dance, we find Maxine Sheets elaborating on Susanne Langer's and Ernst Cassirer's conceptions of aesthetics. Dance is understood by Sheets as a prereflective happening, as a part of the immediate world of lived experience. Dance as art, however, is not a part of the feeling, historical reality of everyday life. It is a symbolic creation of illusions of reality, dance being a creation of an illusion of force, of virtual and not actual force. It is not itself feeling, for the performing artist or the attentive audience. It is a symbol of feeling, of pure feeling, abstracted from the continuum of form in everyday life with its continuum of feeling. It, the dance as art or art generally, is a moment or a set of indivisible, unified moments in the performance or work wherein the symbolic expressions of pure feeling are contained in the form itself.

Does not dance and most art happen after periods of intense preparation? Yes, intensive study, training, and reflection are characteristic of the preliminary, preaesthetic practice periods. But if

84

reflection on the part of either performer or enraptured spectator were to enter during dance itself, we might have education, criticism, or, we presume, even philosophy—not art.

We do not find congenial that notion that purely prereflective and purely abstracted feeling can exist in created or constructed symbolic forms. It seems to us a contradiction to imagine symbols being inherent in naïve to sophisticated artworks "before any kind of reflection whatsoever takes place." But even if Husserl's intuitive method is accepted, we would find it more sensible to regard dance, the symbolic creation of illusions, not as a purely aesthetic experience in the sense of sensuous forms, or forms-in-the-making, symbolically expressive of human feelings—of gloom or joy, terror or peace, anguish, love or fear. Forms or forms-in-the-making of whatever art are better understood not in such a limited conception of creation, presentation, and intuition. Why not, as we prefer to do, understand these aesthetic moments, works, or performances as including and sustainable by facets of enlightenment, of politics, of social relations, and even of economic provisioning?

It seems to us that to regard any of these matters as outside or free of the creation of illusions of reality or of symbolic forms of sensuous expression is a mistake. We think it better to regard aesthetic purity as experiential, as an experience of *human* beings that is possible once human history starts only because other such integral facets are present even though stylized and held almost constant.

We say *almost* constant because the variations may be so small as to be imperceptible during a creation, presentation, or intuition of an artwork. But however subsidiary in consciousness or however buried within or below consciousness, we think it vital that there are flows of signs, of information, of enlightenment between and among the dancers or between dancer and audience. Nor can there ever be a political vacuum. Even if upstaging and other informal, competitive political-influence relations are eliminated, a political pattern of self-control and mutual cooperation must be present to sustain the artistic or aesthetic experience. Social relations are also always present, and the fact that dancers do not dine while dancing does not make their economic sustenance or provisioning irrelevant or not present. None of these facets of the aesthetic experience can be adequately waved away or substituted for by the magic words "lived experience," "prereflective awareness," "intuition," or even the prestigious "aesthetic" or the notion of pure phenomena of feeling.

What we have said about aesthetics and art applies to the equally mundane and sublime fact of the eating of food by human beings. Indeed, the eating of food by people can never be simply a fact. It is always a human experience. This means that it is done with the belief that it is something more or something other than animallike ingestion or a machinelike fueling process. This belief, of course, may range from unconscious to clearly, even brilliantly conscious.

Animals eat, people dine. People may dine in warm human surroundings, with civility, dignity, and grace; with music and art; or they may dine in a grubby, lonely, miserable state. At neither extreme nor in between should the act, the moments, the process, or the practice of eating by humans ever be regarded, however, as only or primarily "economic."

But there are food industries just as there are housing industries. There are special parts of institutions that are, indeed, symbolized as only or primarily engaged in the economic actions or processes of production (and/or distribution) of food as an economic "thing." Are not some people engaged in the economic activities of providing food? Are we not aware of the often foul and difficult work of people laboring in stockyards, in meat-packing plants, or even in traditional but back-breaking farming operations that are not yet automated? Are we not aware of the economic exploitation of the class that sweats so that other classes may dine in the aforementioned idyllic conditions?

Our response is the same as with house production. The generally accepted conception of such human activitity as an economic-institutional practice is a denial of reality. When people engage in food production, as in production of any other things, they are also engaged, by the fact of their humanity, in an ensemble of social relations, political relations, and, indeed, educational relations. The social relations may range from isolation to social integration. The workers may regard themselves as being politically suppressed or oppressed or repressed, they may feel the opposite, or they may feel themselves to be entirely outside the political domain. If either of the former, they may be right or wrong. If the last, they may be merely mistaken or in a state of false consciousness; they cannot be correct. Despite the signs and symbols to the contrary and despite their apparent efficacy in many cases, a person cannot bring into being a partialized reality when he or she is by nature in a total holistic reality.

Actually, as we suggested earlier, it is inappropriate to speak of social relations, political relations, and educational relations. This manner of speaking is traditional and calls up just the wrong images of institutionally distinct human relations. Human interactions do take place in variously symbolized spaces, and people may and do perceive their interactions as discrete or transinstitutional in character. Nor do we mean to suggest that false consciousness is without some positive implications today or that historically it was merely destructive in its human consequences. Our effort here is essentially to reinforce the idea that institutions are not intrinsically or actually specialized, as assumed, despite the special language, operations, or practices that separate one from another institutional enterprise.

One of the magnificent contributions to humanity brought about by such false consciousness, by the understanding of institutions as value-specific, as specialized, was the concentration it permitted. People could preoccupy themselves with certain aspects of their experience while glossing over or becoming unconscious of other aspects. Thus it was that various material goods and services, including medical and health services, education, and science, could develop their increasingly rational, efficient, and economic means of organization, to use Dahl's terms. And we would not suggest that historically institutional thinking was not a great truth for people, given the preceding truth that so much Malthusian misery was fated to be by the iron laws of life, of destiny, of God.

The goodness and power of truths, at least of many truths, may change over time. Even Marx, when urging an end to the division of labor, acknowledged although often backhandedly that it did represent human progress. He spoke grudgingly, for example, of the better work in science and art that resulted from organization of labor "based on modern division of labour [that] still lead only to extremely limited results, *representing a step forward* only compared with the previous narrow isolation.'' (Emphasis added.)[6]

This concentration permitted groups of people to work and become proficient together, often to become professionals and to develop the specialized language, tools, and practices that permitted more highly skilled and effective projects to be carried out in the world. But it is precisely to the extent that divisions of labor were successful and extended not only into every nook and cranny of the so-called economy but also into all other institutionalized domains of modern society that the harmless fiction about an institution's nature being concerned with a particular need and value began to create ever greater negative consequences for humanity.

That little white lie became transformed over time into a major foundation of the modern world. What appears to have happened, quite apart from the often bemoaned or applauded growth in the proportion of public over private space, is the development of institutions to the point that personal, presumably residual, everyday-life space became a shred of what it used to be. Despite a great reduction in working time, giant institutions seem to have moved in and around people until people can hardly breathe in noninstitutionalized everyday-life air.

The increasing institutionalization of personal, city, national, and international space came also from the second major delusion about institutions to which we have referred in passing, namely, that they are suprapersonal. It is time to speak to this delusion. Institutions seem, to many if not most people in modernity, thinglike realities, entities that are a kind of mosaic of hard objects and more ethereal spiritlike substances. The more people have been brought into modern, urban, educated civilization, the more they share this belief. People operate in institutions, but the latter are more than their constituents at any time, have a longevity far beyond that of any set of constituent members, and have a mixed kind of enduring natural and supranatural reality.

Such a belief in the suprahuman substantiality of institutions may be just that, a general belief, or it may take the form of more specific ideas and images. However general or specific, such a belief in the suprapersonal nature of institutions is a most important aspect of the double and false consciousness of which we spoke.

Government nicely illustrates the idea that if an institution exists, then a suprapersonal entity exists—that government is more than the persons in and of government. Government presumably has an existence through time that makes *it* a real *thing*. Take the often-heard phrase, a democratic government is a government of laws and not of men. That notion and Montesquieu's "spirit of the laws" and the "majesty" of the law and the blindfolded goddess of justice contribute to the creation of an atmosphere for generating and reinforcing belief in the eternal, even magical qualities of governmental institutions. Central to the meaning of the phrase "a government of laws, not of men" is the idea that there exists, apart from particular people, a constitution, laws, doctrines, and the like that give government its suprapersonal character. But after stripping away illusions, we find that such an idea is meaningless. It is only people who can give meaning to government and laws. Continuity passes from people to people. The inanimate objects, whether they be weapons, historically revered shields, symbols of the republic, or words written in old statutes or in a constitution, are made meaningful only by living men and women.

These people indeed may have been influenced, through their upbringing or schooling, by what people long dead said, wrote, or did. Of course, the words uttered or written; the poems, songs, or flags made; the adventures and ventures of some people were more striking than were those of others. But currently politically significant objects or products are like all other objects or products in the sense that they constitute potentials whose significance is actualizable only by contemporary people.

Influence is a matter of at least two people actively participating through some kind of direct or indirect connection, whether the process is termed "politics," "education," "social relations," or "art." It is possible, however roughly, to make some assessment of differential degrees of influence and/or merely of status over generations of time, but this possibility does not make government greater than the people who are currently responsible for governing; these are the people who are responsible for according status to the words and deeds of the others already departed. They may continue respected interpretations, extend traditions, or be revisionists or disrespectful rejecters. Government always consists of laws and of living people. Indeed, laws do not have meaning apart from people. The latter of course perform their various inherited operations and speak their special languages developed over centuries, but regardless of where and when these originated they are meaningless unless used and signified currently.

When we ask ourselves whether citizens share in the responsibility of governing even though they are presumably outside government, we must answer affirmatively. The phrase "law-abiding citizen" underlines the importance of the status the citizen gives to the laws and to government officials. Again, whether passively or actively and despite the symbols that put them outside the institution of government, ordinary citizens are involved in the process of government. Our position is, in fact, that all citizens are inside the institution of government at all times despite the widespread consensus by officials and citizens alike that the latter are outside. That belief is a central feature of the aforementioned false institutional consciousness.

When people regard themselves not only as subject to the actions of others with whom they do not share common institutional membership but also as subject to the weight of suprapersonal institutions, especially when this weight is felt as heavy, oppressive, is it any wonder that the mark of modernity increasingly comes to be not only hierarchically partialized individuals in an institutionally divided society but also nonparticipant people? The pervasive so-called apathy is not really indifference but a sense of impotence before suprahuman powers whose human agents seem increasingly incapable of being understood or being anything but oppressive.

Can any distinctions be made between the governors and the governed if everyone is regarded as participating in governing and government? Yes, indeed. It is precisely the social-psychological reality—the human languages, operations, and encompassing practices—that makes of the former something greater than the latter, that gives to government its special rights and potential powers. Government officials are different from citizens precisely because the former are symbolized as such, as members of and within government. They are symbolized as people who have the right to participate in the making and/or execution of certain decisions while other persons have no legitimate right to so participate. And unlike mere citizens, the President's men have just as much special right and duty to protect the nebulous Office of the President as all the King's men have to protect the equally spectral Crown. In fact, all institutional distinctions rest on just such a social-psychological foundation.

We do not intend to denigrate this foundation. We do not regard it as trivial. But we do intend to indicate that such a foundation exists only to the extent that living people act toward themselves and others in the appropriate membership-nonmembership manner. In other words, no institutions can be imagined to have an existence apart from or beyond the life spans of particular people. Institutions are renewed and re-created constantly, as people live through time and as some people are succeeded by other people. Despite assertions by philosophers to the contrary, the abstract cannot exist apart from the concrete or the general apart from the particular.

It may appear to the reader that we are belaboring an obvious point, but the modern world is filled with illusory and delusory apparitions: collectivities that have come to be real instead of merely denoting people in their relations over particular time periods in particular places. Governments with a capital "G" exist, Societies exist, Economies exist, and even Classes exist—each with a suprapersonal reality and its distinct pattern of activity or practice. And these supposedly most substantial suprapersonal entities or, in sociological language, these "macrolevel collectivities," presumably have ghostly skeletons termed "structures" inside them. The structures somehow give birth to or *are* the essentials of the collectivities and give them durability through time; when structural change occurs, the collectivity itself changes. We regard such structural theory and analysis as a modern equivalent of witchcraft.[7]

People do act in a partialized manner, although they are not partialized people. Some people wear black robes and use law books while others wear blue or red uniforms and carry guns or fire-fighting equipment. The development of consensual codes about who does what under what circumstances has indeed brought civilization some of its finest moments and monuments, but it has also prepared the way for such a partialization of people and problems that people will no longer be sufficiently flexible to meet the new challenges of potential ecological disasters, massive personality breakdowns and violence, and nuclear holocausts.

The twin delusions about institutions have facilitated and been facilitated by the development of the concept that the partialized person needs, values, and is capable of taking in *services*. The hierarchically divided institutions have become in overall form the service society. This is more than merely a matter of so-called welfare services, for the specially disadvantaged of modern societies—such as blacks in America and especially black youths, the elderly, women segregated by housebound roles, and poor people of whatever color, age, or sex. All people, including the most affluent, and all institutions operate as if they were collections of parts each needing or providing a distinct service or set of services. The idea that some people are inside and others outside particular institutions not only prepares the ground for the idea that government's special task and competence is to provide citizens with a range of public services. The idea goes far beyond the institution of government.

The presumably separated, specialized institutions of medical health care are regarded as exclusive communities, having as members only subsets of the members of society. Take, for example, the idea that only qualified people are members of medical/health-care institutions. In other words, "laymen" who are not properly certified are not regarded as practitioners of medicine. But a moment's reflection will show that that idea is wrong. It is nonsensical for the patient or potential patient, you or me, to be regarded as not actively involved in practicing both preventive and curative medicine, sometimes alone, as an amateur, and sometimes in concert with professionally trained doctors and others.

Can anyone really imagine the medical institution, the medical community, as one to which we do not belong? Do we not observe

92

and remark upon our own symptoms? Do we not take our own temperatures? Do we not engage in programs of diet and exercise that constitute preventive medicine? Do we not cooperate actively with our doctors in embarking on a regime of drug taking that they may prescribe but in which we participate, passively or actively, as total persons?

The prevailing notion is exactly opposite: There is a medical community outside which are patients or clients who are serviced by the community members inside. The notion of ''service'' is crucial. Not only are people treated as laymen; also as ''patients'' they are reduced to objects that are less than totally human, that are bodies or parts of bodies or minds. We potential or actual patients are regarded as subhuman machines needing servicing. The plethora of social services are addressed to the same kinds of partialized and objectified persons; the quasi-religious idea of service has been converted into a relationship stripped of a truly interpersonal connotation.

Those from within the exclusive community are something *more* than merely persons: they are professional people or technically qualified people. The others, the people outside the community who are serviced, are something *less* than people: they are not only beyond (below) *the* community, that is, the professional community; they are also partialized and therefore less than total persons. The partialization of specialists acquires a suprapersonal aura for themselves and for the lowly beholders or recipients of the service, as the specialists seem to partake of the suprapersonal character of the institution.

The idea of a service is one in which many well-meaning persons take some pride. Participating in providing or improving social services or services to the elderly or the poor, for example, is something that is thought to give humanity to an increasingly mechanical, heartless society of economic functioning. To many participants, or at least to those still idealists among them, it is important to maintain a truly total image of the person receiving the service. The problem is sometimes posed as to how to extend a range of services to ensure that the total range of needs of given kinds of people are met.

The problem is perhaps a subtle one. The idea of a person as

93

having needs implies that a person is not quite a subject but, rather, an object. The person as object is viewed as consisting of parts. The total range of needs would include the proper functioning of each part as well as the total personal system. But those people who concentrate on one part or need of a person, even though providing more or better inputs for proper functioning of this person, are alienated; they are distanced from the person who is being serviced. The person so serviced must also be alienated and distanced.

A person serviced is a person who receives something often made or prepared anonymously, usually standardized, and certainly not something in which he or she has participated except passively, as a recipient. However unintended, a service-providing person's image of the other person demeans the other. It prevents the person servicing from experiencing as a total person with the other just as it ordinarily prevents the person serviced from experiencing as a total person with the former. When we speak of service-providing persons and persons serviced we have in mind the professionalized, institutionally specialized kinds of servicing that are so labeled and not the informal human services people often provide each other as total persons. Of course, in the so-called service professions there occasionally are persons who have a true consciousness and sometimes meet persons being serviced who have the same consciousness. Extraordinary personal relations—even friendships—are created on rare occasions.

Does such a happening mean that there is a need for "humanizing" the provision of services? Not so long ago there was a not so different effort to insert "human relations" into the dehumanizing factory. In fact, that attempt is made in many factories as well as in schools and institutes of so-called labor-management relations. But humanizing particular services, particular institutional settings, or even an entire institution is impossible. It is impossible because such humanizing does not and cannot treat of total people at the same time it treats of particularized services, with their discrete institutional origins. Humanizing means cutting through or passing over or somehow opening institutions that are so exclusive and esoteric that they do not allow for human relations, for total-person relations.

Opening institutions is both more and less difficult than one might imagine. It is more difficult to the extent that delusory institutional thinking is embedded in the kinds of sacred beliefs that are the framework of the modern false consciousness. These beliefs constitute a kind of system of axioms or coordinates used by modern people to map and locate themselves in their human world. These beliefs have their counterparts in beliefs about the nature of the physical world. We generally regard the world as flat even though we know it is round. We regard the stars we see as really being there when, actually, many have burned out long ago but the time it takes for light to travel to us from them makes it appear that they have a current existence. We ordinarily assume that the sun rises when in fact the earth moves in relation to the sun. None of these assumptions or seeming realities, which conflict with actual reality, do very much damage unless people act on them in such a way as to damage themselves or others or lose the ability to find practical solutions to real problems.

Opening institutions is less difficult than one might imagine because of the nature of their reality vis-à-vis everyday life. Let us examine that real state of affairs carefully now.

If the human projects in a modern society were listed in terms of their "sponsoring" or parent institutions, one would end up with a long list of projects described in the less than total-person terms used by each specialized institution. There would be a remainder of smaller-scale, mini- or microprojects that exist at the sub- or extrainstitutional level. This is sometimes referred to as the level of everyday life.[8] In fact, as we suggested already, it is at the level of everyday life that total persons exist knowing themselves and each other as such. Even there, though, modern people are increasingly subject to the partializing signs and symbols that enter from the language of one or another specialized institution. But is such everyday-life space outside or under institutional space? Can and does the latter invade or overlap to some extent with the former? Or are they in reality a unitary space?

"Everyday life" in a restrictive first instance is definable and defined only by persons themselves. Thus, what is one person's everyday life is another person's specialized work or profession.

What is one man's everyday life is carried on only from Saturday night to Monday morning, while another's is a twenty-four-hour-a-day, seven-days-a-week everyday-life space and everyday-life time. Working women and housewives may—or may not—feel that they have no everyday life or that their everyday life is totally penetrated by their working life.

A more conventional but we think also restricted view is that everyday life takes place in those spaces and places and at those times when the more formally organized institutions (such as government, the school, the factory, or the office) do not claim the person. Everyday life takes place either in noninstitutional spaces or in the more informally organized social institutions. These would include the family in the apartment, friends on the street corner or in the bar, and other such informally organized settings. These are viewed as the central nodes in this sense of everyday life.

People of institutional consciousness understand the world to be in such separable domains, one of everyday life and the other of (more) organized institutional life. People of double consciousness understand or sense these as coexisting, co-present domains. Everyday life in this second instance, then, is one part of a dichotomy. The other is institutional(alized) life. We find such a dichotomy to be wrong: we think there is but one domain with two (or more) faces. In reality, despite what people believe, *all life is everyday life*. We must examine more carefully projects that presumably occur not in everyday life but under the aegis or in the domain of institutions These are the so-called institutional projects, which we find are misunderstood because of several kinds of errors.

The French scholar Henri Lefebvre is known for his appreciation of so-called everyday life. His conception of everyday life seems to be what we termed the more conventional view, but he verges on the last mentioned sense of everyday life as the total social space of everyone, at least after institutions are demystified. Let us quote from Lefebvre at length when he speaks of our current dilemmas:

Either [italics added] we exert all our energy (such energy as every individual qua social individual possesses) in consolidating existing institutions and ideologies—State, Church, philosophical systems or political organizations—whilst attempting to consolidate the quotidian on which these ''superstructures'' are established and maintained; *or* we reduce these entities (state, church, culture, etc.) to their true proportions, we refuse to see them and we revalue the mere residuum upon which they are built—everyday life; *either* we elect to serve ''causes'' *or* we support the humble cause of everyday life.[9]

He comes very close to saying that all of life is everyday life: ''Yet people are born, live and die. They live well or ill; but they live in everyday life, where they make or fail to make a living either in the wider sense of surviving or not surviving, or just surviving or living their lives to the full. It is in everyday life that they rejoice and suffer; here and now.''[10] In speaking to the presumed objections of the specialized social sciences, history, and philosophy to the claim that everyday life has special status, Lefebvre makes the following rejoinder: ''We are about to undertake a fairly important inquiry into facts that philosophy has hitherto overlooked and the social sciences have arbitrarily divided and distributed. Indeed the experts of specialized sciences tend to isolate facts to their own conveniences, classifying them according to categories that are both empirical and distinct.''[11]

Yet Lefebvre somehow manages to hold on to a kind of distinctness, at least to a kind of analytic distinctness, between modernity and everyday life. He poses them as polar opposites, although connected. Everyday life and modernity have:

. . . simultaneity and their connection. The quotidian is what is humble and solid, what is taken for granted and that of which all the parts follow each other in such a regular, unvarying succession . . . ; the modern . . . stands for what is novel, brilliant, paradoxical and bears the imprint of technicality and worldliness . . . it is art and aestheticism—not readily discernible in so-called modern spectacles or in the spectacles the modern world makes of itself to itself . . . [while the quotidian] is the ethics underlying routine and the aesthetics of familiar settings.[12]

Lefebvre asks, ''Is there a world-scale tendency towards

homogeneity in everyday life and 'modernism' or on the contrary towards their differentiation?"[13]

Our point is that Lefebvre, while contributing a most innovative current to encrusted Marxist thought, seemed finally unable to make the next, conclusive step of conceiving everyday life to consist of all of life, marked by more or less modern (divided, specialized, institutionalized) features. Perhaps the importance to him of, and his hopes for, everyday life made it impossible for him to go on to recognize institutional consciousness for what and where it is, namely, of and in everyday life. Thus, he was unable to deny the existence of institutions, in the sense in which both scholars and people in everyday life attributed to them a separate, discrete reality. But it is precisely in everyday life that institutions are given the illusion of having specialized substance, suprapersonal solidity, continuity and consequence beyond the persons constituting them in any time period.

The concept of everyday life was most important to Lefebvre. It was necessary in order for him to develop Marxist thought in more fruitful directions. The following quotations are also in point to the earlier mentioned classic Marxist position on the primacy of economic needs and activities. The person in everyday life, in fact, becomes for Lefebvre, without his so stating it in these words, the crucial total entity, the crucial total unit. The total person is the unit that is not and cannot be treated as divided, as having discrete needs, as having needs that can be matched to specialized institutions. Let us quote again from Lefebvre to illustrate all this:

> Production is not merely the making of products: the term signifies on the one hand "spiritual" production, that is to say creations (including social time and space) and on the other material production or the making of things: it also signifies the self-production of a "human being" in the process of historical self-development, which involves the production of social relations. Finally . . . the term embraces *reproduction,* not only biological . . . but the material reproduction of the tools of production, of technical instruments and of social relations into the bargain . . . this many-faceted phenomenon that affects objects and beings, which controls nature and adapts it to humanity, this *praxis*

and *poiesis* does not take place in the higher spheres of a society (state, scholarship, "culture") but in everyday life."[14]

Finally:

> Ideologies are made of understanding and interpretations . . . of the world and knowledge plus a certain amount of illusion, and might bear the name of "culture." A culture is also a *praxis* or a means of distributing supplies in a society and thus directing the flow of production; it is in the widest sense a means of production, a source of ideologically motivated actions and activities. This active role of ideologies had to be reinstated in the Marxist plan in order to prevent its degenerating into philosophism and economism; the notion of production then acquires its full significance as production by a human being of his own existence. Furthermore, consumption thus reenters the plan as dependent upon production and with the specific mediation of ideology, culture, institutions and organizations. . . . There is a feed-back . . . within determined production relations (capitalism) between production and consumption, structures and superstructures, scholarship and ideology. . . . *Everyday life emerges as the sociological point of feed-back* [italics added]; this crucial yet much disparaged point has a dual character; it is *residuum* (of all the possible specific and specialized activities outside social experience) and the *product* of society in general; it is the point of delicate balance and that where imbalance threatens. A revolution takes place when and only when, in such a society, people can no longer lead their everyday lives; so long as they can live their ordinary lives relations are constantly re-established."[15]

Most scholars, however, as most other people, are in a kind of double consciousness at best and are not even as clear as Lefebvre on the reality and potential importance of everyday life. When they restrict the term to so-called private, personal spaces and times, they make a basic error. This error is the corollary of the erroneous analytic decomposition of total persons into parts followed by attention being given only to the parts and not to the whole. Such reductionism is accompanied by another, nearly opposite kind of error: that of reification. This is the error of conceiving as the basic entities in the social world not persons or sets of persons but suprapersonal collectivities, including the institutions themselves.

99

The result of such a complex of errors is the dichotomy between institutions and everyday life.

The presumed properties of partialized persons and of suprapersonal institutions together produce the subject matter of the institutional projects. The remaining space of total persons for everyday-life projects is diminished even further as institutions, through their projects, seemingly encroach more and more upon everyday life. The image of the person in everyday-life moments having to evade an institutional presence that may have extended almost overnight into one's neighborhood or even one's home seems familiar to all of us. Despite the familiar resonance, the image is misleading and it generates undue pessimism.

The image is misleading because the conventional wisdom is wrong which implies that when a total person moves from everyday-life into institutional space (say, into working, economic institutional space) the person somehow loses totality by putting on certain clothing or a uniform and becoming known by a job classification or organizational title. For every man and woman the world of work, the week of work, the wages in kind or in other symbolic payment are a vital part of their everyday lives. When at work or anyplace else, the person remains total despite the practices that surround him or her, practices often designed to give people a machinelike sense of identity or even a sense of being components or cogs in a machine.

In fact, the everyday-life world is infused with strands and threads of specialized language, operations, and practices brought there by total persons, in person or via the mass media, who move from their institutional to their more personalized, private spaces and vice versa. So, too, is the most specialized of institutional domains filled with presumably unspecialized language and practices of supposedly separated everyday life.

If the two were indeed a dichotomy, the institutional and everyday-life spaces, we would be facing a more difficult future than we are. We would have, and many people think we do have, numerous problems of somehow connecting these disjointed spaces. Fortunately, there is but one domain although it contains various

100

distinct practices and often requires people to perform various practices or play several roles as if they were not total people, a feat not without its destructive consequences for people. To examine this matter of everyday and institutional life, let us spend a few moments on the institution often thought of as the prototypical opposite, indeed, the contradiction, of everyday life, namely, science.

Science as an institution (or the sciences as a set of institutions) somehow exists above and beyond particular people in history. Like all modern institutions but even more than most, it is a project(s) special and specialized. Supposedly it deals with one or more aspects of the world in a manner that ordinary men and women do not in their everyday lives.

Let us examine this key claim briefly. If we find that science has no greater claim than any other institution to exclusivity, we will be in a position to assess the entire rationale of divided institutions and the divisions of labor and life that form the dominant modern landscape.

The usual claim by philosophers of science is that science differs from other domains in terms of having at its core a special method, the scientific method. It is asserted, at the very least, that that method differs from common sense. As a philosopher of science, Ernest Nagel, put it:

> It is the desire for explanations which are at once systematic and controllable by factual evidence that generates science and it is the organization and classification of knowledge on the basis of explanatory principles that is the distinctive goal of the sciences . . . it is a quest for explanatory hypotheses that are genuinely testable, because they are required to have logical consequences precise enough not to be compatible with almost every conceivable state of affairs. The hypotheses sought must therefore be subject to the possibility of rejection, which will depend on the outcome of critical procedures, integral to the scientific quest, for determining what the actual facts are.[16]

Thus, for Nagel as for many others, science is understood as a qualitatively very different project from those in which persons engage or live in everyday life. Science is presumably not part of mundane, everyday life but of a very specialized and separate set

101

of life moments and periods. "Common sense," the kind of thinking people do in everyday life, supposedly is different because it does not use the scientific mode of inquiry: "The conclusions of science, unlike common-sense beliefs, are the products of scientific method . . . the difference between the cognitive claims of science and common sense . . . stems from the fact that the former are the products of scientific method."[17]

Advocates of the special character not only of scientific institutions but also of science as a mode of being in the world stress its systematic and reflective nature. Our own view is that scientists and nonscientists alike may range in their life-styles and life moments from very systematic to chaotic or random or whatever the opposite condition may be called. So, too, do we think that most people in their common-sense spaces, places, and moments search for explanatory hypotheses, test hypotheses, determine facts, and accept uncritically and even often unselfconsciously various concepts, premises, assumptions, understandings, and theories about the nature of the world. But as soon as we say this about ordinary people in everyday life, we immediately say it also of scientists in their professional pursuits.

How many if any scientists can really take into conscious and considered account in their work all the matters crucial to establishing validity which would constitute a "genuine test" of a hypothesis? Scientists have to take much on faith—just as do nonscientists. They must assume the correctness of much work in their own field; they must trust authorities, albeit authorities in and of science and not of governmental or religious institutions. Entire ontologies, that is, sets of assumptions and theories of the nature of being, of existence, of what "things" exist, must be taken on faith by the experimental scientist. Scientists must suspend judgment about many things. And they do not rationally take account of all relevant matters and then reasonably exercise their informed judgments about what to accept certainly as true, what to accept provisionally as true, what to treat as neither true nor false, and the like. They, like ordinary nonscientist people, are mixtures of prejudices and biases, of information and ignorance, of insight and stupidity.

102

What, precisely, does separate science from everyday, common-sensical life? It is precisely what separates government officials from citizens, doctors from patients, attorneys from clients. As we said in the case of government as institution, the heart of the matter is social-psychological. But we did not say quite enough with that phrase. We underline again that the world is partializable into domains by means of differentiable language, operations, tools, and practices. In the case of the modern institutions of science, what separates them from commonsensical, everyday life and from other specialized institutions is just such sustained, self-conscious concerns with limited parts of the world. That sustained self-conscious concern can exist as a specialized human enterprise in the manifold of everyday-life concerns of people only by means of the development of professional/technical language and operations.

There is nothing special or unique about science or scientists beyond their very human ability to make, to learn, and to become more or less proficient in the specific language and operations that constitute their closed community. With the stabilization of any such set of human linguistic and operational practices, development of theoretical understanding and of ideas, always tested in the crucible of the practical physical and human worlds, proved to be possible in a more or less additive if not orderly fashion. Periodically it was not additive, and disorder occurred when tried and apparently true models were found to be wanting compared with newer and quite different ideas about how things were or how they worked.

But a basic belief of many scientists and other people is that science has a natural monopoly on true knowledge, on real enlightenment, which is rooted in essential, innate needs of all people for knowledge and in the differential talents of people for practicing science. Those who argue for such a natural division of science from other human pursuits often do recognize that it is impossible to clearly specify the dividing line between scientific and commonsensical knowledge or thinking. Although he concludes that there is "at least a core of firm meaning for each of these words" (common sense" and "scientific"), Nagel is quite unclear on the key questions thereby begged.[18] These questions concern the nature of the dividing line that separates science from common sense. How firm is it? How much of a barrier is it? How permeable is it? How may people cross it: by learning language and operations acknowledged as scientific or by trying to employ the scientific method in their everyday, commonsensical domains? "Common-sense beliefs are not subjected, as a matter of established principle, to systematic scrutiny in the light of data secured for the sake of determining the accuracy of those beliefs and the range of their validity."[19] How established must the principle be? How systematic must the scrutiny be? Nagel admits that "no sharp line separates beliefs generally subsumed under the familiar but vague rubric of 'common-sense' from those cognitive claims recognized as 'scientific.' "[20] The boundary is "notoriously hazy." However, Nagel's preference, indeed, his profession, is to emphasize speciality, separation, and distinction ("these words do in fact connote important and recognizable differences"). Our purpose, to the contrary, is to emphasize commonality and similarity. We allow, of course, for differences among institutional and human projects but not for the kind of categorical divergence between downgraded prescientific, presumably nonreflective human activities attributed to common people in everyday life and the special practices that presumably mark scientific inquiries or products and only scientific inquiries or products.

The philosopher Maurice Natanson, of an existential and phenomenological persuasion, distinguishes science from philosophy and both from everyday life. Acknowledging the thoughts of Edmund Husserl, Jean-Paul Sartre, and especially Alfred Schutz, Natanson's work argues for a distinct domain of science as being in the nature of the world just as much as does the different approach taken by the positivist Nagel. In fact, Natanson's is an argument explaining the grounds for the multiple institutional worlds of man, including the central, not more important, but distinct "common-sense existence" in the "world of daily life" or of "mundane reality," as he often terms it.[21] Although such worlds as art and religion, with their appropriate roles, have other hallmarks, reflection is understood as the distinguishing characteristic of philosophy and science. People playing roles are required to reflect in these worlds in contrast to the world of mundane reality. Philosophy requires persons to bring their unique experiential histories to their roles, whereas science presumably demands something quite different of its practitioners. In fact, science demands impersonality.

Natanson recognizes connections between mundane reality and the specialized worlds of man. However, he stresses the distinctions in such comments as these: "Reflection on the world and on oneself in the world is part of common-sense existence, yet radical, *root* reflection, which is the mark of true philosophizing, is on the far side of daily life."[22] Again, contrasting a person's experience with individual births and deaths in everyday life with the same themes presented in a work of art, Natanson comments, "Of course, the similarities are there, but they fade to nothing in comparison with the shattering quality of the art originals."[23]

Natanson's argument essentially stresses differences and distinctness among everyday-life and other human roles and worlds whereas our position stresses the similarities, the interpenetration and the simultaneity of moments. His is in the tradition of analysis, albeit phenomenological analysis, whereas ours is attempting to postulate not synthesis so much as a more holistic, unified approach to human life and the human world.

For Natanson, as for many other phenomenologists, the world is fundamentally divisible into an everyday-life world and an institutional world, the latter a world of "great symbolic systems and constructions." If the intention were to stress that human experiences could be categorized as unreflective taking-things-for-granted or reflective we would have no great quarrel. But Natanson, as do others, speaks of the world of everyday life in terms of "the taken-for-grantedness of everyday life." Despite the acknowledgment that institutions begin in everyday life, everyday life remains effectively a world of total unreflectiveness, a residual even if basic region of somewhat less than human or of quasi-human stimulus-and-response.

It would have to be admitted that institutional reflection surrounds and sometimes may even be temporarily replaced by the prereflective lived experiential movements and actions of persons in or from the everyday-life world. Little attention, of course, has been paid to how such movements between worlds occur or whether, once within the institutional domain, the prereflectiveness only seems like everyday-life experience. Ironically, it took an extreme logical positivist, a behaviorist, a B. F. Skinner, to extend throughout the institutional world as well as the world of everyday life a specific model of a person as just that: a behaving interface between stimulus and response.

The reader will remember how the earlier phenomenological treatment of dance posited worlds of art and everyday life both having the core characteristic of prereflective, intuitive lived experiences. But art was separated from everyday life. It was separated because art was the expression of illusions in various symbolized forms. Thus, in art feelings were abstract and symbolized, not directly real as in everyday life. In contrast to the affective context of everyday life, wherein prereflective awareness (of body and bodily movement) is supported by actual feeling, "The dance is a symbol of a form of human feelings and is presented by a symbol of the human who feels those feelings in everyday life."[24] Perhaps the key reason, though, that dance as art takes place outside everyday life is that dance lacks a history: "it has no past, and in terms of the very last movement, it has no future."[25] Sheets concludes: "Apart from its creation and presentation, the dance has no spatial-temporal existence. It is apparent, then, that the temporality and spatiality of the dance, while founded upon the lived experience of time and space in everyday life, are structures within the total structures of the illusion which dance creates."[26]

Our disagreement is twofold. First, why is it necessary to separate illusions from everyday life? Doing this impoverishes and violates the nature of everyday life as we intuit or apprehend it. Trying to suspend our own preconceptions leads us in the direction of seeing art and artistic illusions as part and parcel of everyday life.

The second disagreement is with the notion that art or at least dance does not exist in everyday life because it has an ephemeral existence. So, too, do many things unquestionably within everyday life. And extending the point to all art does not change things. What in everyday life has spatial-temporal existence apart from its creation and presentation? Even more to the point is that we believe dance as art, works of dance as works of all the so-called arts, do have histories. Treating them as phenomena in and of themselves does not bother us, but cutting them off from their perhaps not so artistic precedents, including their reflective precedents, so as to give them a special non-everyday-life status does bother us. It is as unsatisfactory as taking all things that have a reflective characteristic out of everyday life. It is not necessary or good to remove dance if not all art as well as science and philosophy from everyday life, as phenomenologists in concert seem to have done.

Although the two camps of phenomenologists and positivist scientists seem to view one another as enemies, they both have given support to an institutional consciousness that unduly diminishes the residual everyday-life world. One of our theses, in fact, is that the modern consciousness has become a kind of unreflective, if not prereflective, consciousness and is most unreflective in the largest sense on the part of people who are the most involved in the presumably most reflective, non-everyday-life institutional sectors of our society.

We have cited Natanson here because much of his thinking and that of his existential and phenomenological predecessors and peers is true and good. But by making the mundane world not quite so mundane and permitting less rigid dividing lines among worlds and roles, we think the incredibly difficult and increasingly impossible task of persons in moving from one to another role can be replaced by another difficult but possible and, indeed, enjoyable project. This project is to have people simultaneously pursue their everyday life and their exotic confrontations and engagements, meld their naïve, commonsensical, mundane pursuits with their specialized pursuits, and try to merge the sacred and the profane. If a final fusion proves impossible or forever unreachable, at least the exotic will take place within the mundane and not on its far side or beyond its orbit.

We have belabored a point that to many readers will be obvious and not need affirmation, namely, that institutions are no more or less than a set of people performing with each other in a set of operations defined and guided by language, operations, and ideas that mark projects as theirs, projects in which outsiders presumably do not participate. But if this point is conceded, it means that institutions may be opened to many or even to all people merely by a change in the appropriate matters of social psychology.

Furthermore, such a conception means that institutional distinctness in operations, language, and ideas is not a matter of differences of kind or method but merely of degree. It is a matter of degree in the use or understanding of the institutionally specific, professional/technical language and modus operandi. It is not the qualitative, categoric difference it is often made out to be. All nonscientists use the so-called scientific method just as all scientists use instinct, intuition, and fantasy. Emotion and reason are always present for scientists and nonscientists alike. For good or bad, artists doing their art and experiencing their so-called aesthetic pleasure are mixing these presumably pure moments with craft and science, just as scientists are actually experiencing artistic pleasure, sometimes intensely.

It is also relevant to note that the so-called natural language of everyday life used by laymen is also used by *scientists as scientists*. Nuclear physicists have themselves stressed how impossible it is to operate in quantum mechanics or with quantum theory, which has concepts and language very different in kind from that of classical physics, without some use of the latter language.[27] Moreover, the natural language developed over the centuries has been very much penetrated by, for example, the language of classical physics. Thus, when we speak of lay language and concepts and of scientific language and concepts, again we refer to differences in the degree, rigor, and self-consciousness with which special language is used in reference to parts or aspects of the world. Contrary to much popular opinion, we do not believe that there is a qualitatively specific scientific thinking or acting different from any other kind of thinking or acting of human beings.

108

If the foregoing is true, then the matter of opening up exclusive institutional communities is only a matter of working on the social psychology involved. It is not a matter of making difficult or impossible alterations in people or in suprahuman institutional entities, nor does it violate a natural and pure division of modes of being in the world.

Distorted consciousness is of course real. Partialization may distort, indeed, has distorted, much of modern consciousness. Such partialization is real although the complexity surrounding it is artificial. The resulting problems are real, although such modern consciousness is false.

Modern institutions are thus a mix of the real and the unreal. They are unreal in a double sense. They are really the suprapersonal collective entities with temporal longevity that they are often thought to be, and they are unreal in the sense that people performing within them are not really as partialized as believed. They are very real in the sense that the actions of a deluded person are real even if he believes he is Jesus Christ or Julius Caesar.

We would argue, then, that a more valid sense of the real world is that instead of being institutionally divided it is a unitary human space marked by nodes of human activities wherein total persons exist despite purposeful or unintentional efforts to partialize them. These nodes of human activities range from relative self-consciously formalized, institutionally symbolized enterprises to less formal, semi- or noninstitutional human projects. The various human projects, whether or not formally institutionalized, range from highly to loosely organized, tightly hierarchical to more decentralized, and so forth. The forms and textures of such a single, encompassing everyday-life space may be variously felt and described—by untrained persons just as by highly trained sociologists.

The wisdom of a belief in a total, overall, encompassing space, whether termed "everyday life" or something else, helps to blunt the otherwise seemingly sharp boundaries among institutions and between institutionalized and noninstitutionalized or less formally institutionalized human practices.

109

The political scientist Harold D. Lasswell and the philosopher Abraham Kaplan have conjointly tried to demystify institutional consciousness about political and governmental institutions, especially the delusion of suprapersonal existence, held by numerous political and other social scientists. Commenting on government and "the state" as institutions, they say:

> Political science . . . deals not with "states" and "governments" but with concrete acts of human beings. . . . The state has been defined as a group of persons whose practices and perspectives exhibit certain observable characteristics. Similarly here we define "government" in terms of the practices of specified persons. . . . Every proposition about the abstraction "state" can be replaced by a set of propositions referring only to the concrete acts of certain persons and groups. And the same is true for the abstraction "government."[28]

And they make a point that holds true far beyond the political institutions to which they refer: "When state and government are conceived in purely abstract terms, they are easily hypostatized and confused with one another."[29] Such a making of supposedly discrete but abstract institutions substantial and real when they are actually multifaceted human projects is done by specialists as well as by ordinary people from all walks of life. It is little wonder that the sacred beliefs of modernity are what they are.

We indicated that becoming mature does not mean learning to live in sequential periods of divided labor and life among and in specialized, partialized moments that presumably discrete institutional domains and organizations provide for modern people. Maturity lies in recognizing that persons of all ages may indeed learn specialized languages and operations relative to partialized aspects of the world so long as the total person's indivisible, nonpartializable experiences remain at the cherished core of the self and in the self's relations to others whatever the human project context. Maturity lies in opening exclusive, partializing institutions.

Unfortunately very little has been said about alternative possibilities even by persons profoundly critical of institutions. Despite his own partial acceptance at least of the then current reality's institutional distinctions, Marx was perhaps the last serious critic of the modern division of labor. He understood it as being the major reason for the development of industrial capitalism as a more effective, efficient, and productive system than its predecessor. And he criticized it in the spirit of anticipating a future based on something other than an increasingly humanly crippling division of labor.

Marx foresaw the possibility of freeing people from the fixed, institutionally defined roles that modern capitalism required. But while he glimpsed the withering away of institutionalized government, he did not quite see how everyday life might be made or reunderstood as capable of becoming a space for total persons living integral human experiential moments (except for a principle of rapid or easy rotation among specialized roles). Few of his self-proclaimed followers spent much time on developing a strategy of opening—and thereby beginning to dissolve—discrete, hard hierarchical and exclusive institutions as we have come to think of them. We shall have occasion to comment further on the current stance of some Marxists in the concluding chapter.

Non-Marxist sociologists as well as others have engaged in criticism of this or that practice or this or that departure from Max Weber's statement of ideal-type bureaucracy in the operations of modern institutions and their organized subsystems. But nearly all take as eternal truth the encrusted notion that human nature requires vertically organized hierarchies. The inescapably hierarchical character of institutions is a third sacred belief in modernity, supporting and being supported by fears of what might happen in terms of breakdown of civilization if discrete, suprapersonal institutions were opened.

Two writers who were profound critics of institutions but who saw no way out are Franz Kafka and Ken Kesey.[30] They represent similar points of view but have a significant difference, perhaps reflecting differences in their historical circumstances. To Kafka, the person is powerless and pitiful before the anonymous leaders of modern institutions. Whether on trial for unknown crimes or in a castle of unknowable cartography, the single person is as in a dream, a nightmare from which there is no escape except self-dissolution and total servitude before the mystifications of the mysterious masters.

To Kesey the person is also alone. But, rather than being power-less and pitiful, the person is prideful and potent—to a point. The person treated as patient, the supposedly insane person, sees the madness and unreality of the supposedly sane. By personal clarity and strength of character this one mature person makes the institution's mystified identity disappear. What is left are only men and women programming themselves to be the guardians of a society filled with really sick people, as sick as they. At the end, the one person who cannot be psychologically manipulated is made less than a man, made a part man–part animal, by being put under the surgeon's knife for a lobotomy. Psychosurgery, not gas chambers, is the civilized society's answer to those who refuse to credit institutional authority, legitimacy, and reality. In the absence of a considered strategy, it would seem that confronting institutions or their defenders is a risky matter at best.

Our point is that strategies for beginning to end the divisions of labor and life have been few and far between. They have varied from the suggestion by Kesey of the necessity and possibility of the hero or, it is hoped, many heros to dissolve delusions, to bring institutional walls down. An awakening into immediate true consciousness and subsequent action is one possible solution, and we do not reject it. But it would be useful to have another solution if possible, because instances of such insightful action are not easily found. Nor do we find sufficient the end-to-institutions-immediately attitude, whether that of a sophisticated Ivan Illich or the posture of smash-the-institutions taken by extremist groups.[31]

Our own suggestion is for a strategy of opening institutions. We shall explain what we mean by this in the next chapter. We must also be prepared to address major objections to any institutional opening up. Does it not entail lowering or dissipating standards: of excellence, of competence, of skill? Are we advocating the end to specialists, to brain surgeons or jet pilots? Are we proposing a kind of dangerous selection by lot of who is to do brain surgery or fly jet aircraft?

If institutions are opened, would not this event violate the still hallowed beliefs that the most important, most basic things are

112

indeed economic, that the pursuit of the economic is the priority human project, and that the economic would be endangered if the institutional fabric of the society began to be unraveled? Should anyone contemplate violation of sacred beliefs and long-lasting human traditions when the consequences seem to be potentially so disastrous?

In the next chapter, we shall speak to such concerns, concerns that may have appeared with the very first statement of the second part of our basic thesis. But the reader who has understood our position knows that these are questions addressed to pseudoproblems. Our point is not that partializing analysis, specialized theories, and applications of natural, physical, or economic science be discarded. Rather it is that unless and until it is understood that such partializations occur within an encompassing everyday life, within human communities that need understanding and fulfillment as communities of total persons rather than as institutionally divided roles, there is little or no chance that human life-sustaining and -creating experiences can become the enveloping human community matrix. Otherwise we face predictably increasingly distorting, fragmenting, and alienating specialization.

We are suggesting more awareness of and attention to the right-hand side of the diagram presented earlier in the chapter, a domain of already existing but too often unrecognized reality. Giving attention to total persons engaging in multifaceted human experiences involving domiciling or dining or whatever means becoming aware of and performing the "economic" in a context of and consideration for the spectrum of human values necessarily and always involved. We do not disregard or propose to destroy the belief that human beings have physical or biological needs for food, clothing, and shelter, even though we think it necessary to reorganize by opening the presently closed and mystified institutional practices of the real and symbolized economy.

5

Opening Institutions and Building Human Community

Our earlier statement of the second part of our thesis was as follows: "It is possible to begin immediately to rebuild human community by arresting and reducing divisions of labor and life. We assert that this can be done in such a way as to even increase the major benefits of our Western scientific/technological civilization." When we said that opening institutions is only a matter of working on the social psychology involved, we did not mean that doing this is either easy or a matter merely of consciousness, of consciousness changing or consciousness raising. By "social psychology" we meant to refer to integral molar units of attitudes/actions (despite encrusted traditions of thinking of the mind and mental orientations as distinct and separable from the body and physical actions). These molar units are experiences of persons, the ways people experience themselves and others. In other words, in what follows we are speaking of opening institutions in more than only a psychological sense.

By suggesting that opening institutions is not easy, we mean to underline several things. One is that there is a long history behind the modern acceptance of institutional specificity and distinctness, including generations of education and socialization in such regard. Another is that it may be as difficult to get institutional outsiders to enter as it will be to get institutional insiders to open their exclusive communities.

In every instance of opening institutions, we envisage much larger numbers of people than now participating and sharing in decision-making processes and power. Sharing of power is rarely or never easy to accomplish, and in modernity it is particularly difficult to imagine people who are traditionally powerless in many domains feeling that they have the right or the competence to enter such decision making even if invited.

We do not mean to suggest or conjure up the image of masses of laymen suddenly or even slowly entering into specialized, highly professional/technical choice making. We have a slightly different image in mind. Because it is not the modal modern image, it is not easy to communicate. But we will try.

People today are divided from each other by their titles and other signs and symbols of their institutionally specific identities. They are separated not only from people in other institutions but also from people in different sections of the same institution. Conversely, people relate to others because they are connected in terms of the partialized projects shaped and given meaning by the institution's project-determining power structure. These latter interpersonal relationships are functional relationships in the sense that people's functions and their relationship to the functional actions of others are determined by the way the project itself is to function. In other words, institutional or subinstitutional projects are definable precisely as the performances, the practices, or the functioning of people who have roles to play in these projects.

Let us for simplicity's sake restrict our thinking to a single nation. When we speak of opening an institution, we mean in the first instance for everyone to understand that he or she and everyone else in the nation is already a member of the particular institution, whether that institution be particularized as government, education, science, medicine, or whatever. By being a "member" we do not mean in the sense of honorific or only symbolic membership or in the sense of merely some kind of psychological self-identification. We mean full-fledged membership in the sense that every person is understood by all other persons to have roles in the most fundamental, elemental sense of actively participating in whatever value(s) processes are considered to be specific to that institution. As total persons, as human beings who are living in potential future as in actual past relations with other persons, all members of a nation are engaged in processes that deserve to be regarded as "educational," as "governmental," as producing or processing scientific knowledge, as health care, as curing, etc.

But let us immediately remember that there is another implication to the notion of "opening" institutions. We imply by the word "opening" not merely opening to a nation's citizens who have no identities other than simply being nonmembers of a given institution. They ordinarily have one or more other institutional identities. Thus, when one institution opens, it opens automatically to the other institutions. It does so because it opens to persons as total persons, and total persons are already engaged in all institutional domains, whether unwittingly or not and whether passively or actively. The multiplicity of modern institutions begins to fuse together into a single institution.

Instead of today's overarching Society (or State), with its distinct, discrete institutions, the more appropriate image after institutional opening occurs may be one of a single institution encompassing everyone. This single institution will have many nodes or centers of participant activity. The nodes should be permeable in a way that today's institutions are not.

We speak of today's America as still a society of mobility. It is. There are people moving up, down, and across hierarchies. People do move from one city to another, from one house to another, even from one occupation or sometimes one religious denomination to another. But ours is a special kind of mobility. Its special character is not remarked on because, we suppose, it seems to be totally natural. That character is of being fixed in a kind of partialized, exclusive unit before and after one exercises the right of mobility.

The opened institutions of which we speak, with their permeable centers, will be characterized precisely by nonexclusivity and a sense of common membership whatever or wherever the center. Today, apart from a periodically fervent, emotional patriotism—and that not for all of us by any means—there is lacking an elemental sense of common identity among Americans. Most Americans have a less than even vague common membership in the human race. They have a most partialized, constricted, and almost empty sense of being together in the restricted, reduced category of citizens of a country. This feeling is due, we suspect, to the dividing, differentiating character of the modern institutional society. The institutional fusion to which we refer would have great importance in pointing a way toward a reinvigorated, renewed sense of community in the broadest meaning rather than in a narrowly nationalistic or imperialistic mode.

These ideas of institutional opening and fusing could be regarded as signifying the end of specialization and of organization, but we mean to imply neither. We mean the end of exclusive institutions as they are conceived in modernity, but we expect that some other, better organizational forms must and will take their place, whether or not they are called "institutions." In fact, the term we suggested before was that of everyday life or something like "human community."

The proliferation of modern institutions has left men and women increasingly without place in time or space for the grand project of relating to each other as total persons. As the specialized institutions are opened, they will begin to be reshaped and to be redesigned relative to the nodes of activity into which all men and women have the inalienable right to enter. They have the right to enter because they are perfectly competent to decide many important matters themselves and with others. These matters concern human values that constitute the matrix for more professional/technical concerns. Nodes of activity that are specialized, that focus on nuclear physics research, on medical and drug experiments, on agricultural innovations, on computer hardware and software construction we anticipate will proceed. We shall not attempt to forecast or imagine how they will proceed. But they will not proceed as do the current exclusive, indeed, exotic, communities of specialists, who are unconnected to and, indeed, uncaring about most other people, including fellow specialists in other institutions.

The masses of people who are toward the lower levels of institutions will profit at once if this most fundamental human right is recognized. This includes many people who are institutionally redundant. They are really outside or below any modern institution, existing as essentially subhuman garbage.

We speak of the right to be inside the human community. By this, we mean that all people would be recognized as capable of participating and sharing in power in the making of numbers of major decisions that concern the very vital fabric of everyday life, of the human community itself. It is a right to self-management in all currently exclusive institutional domains. It is a right not satisfied if exercised only through representatives and only in one institution: government.

Participation in subcommunities of a more human community will be different in character and quality from what may appear to be superficially similar or identical participation in the institutional, professional/technical communities of the developed urban-industrial society. Human welfare and human rights to participate today are partialized and residual matters. At least in North America, but not only there, people who have not been successful in gaining a place in an exclusive community are regarded as at best cases deserving the partialized attention of the various service institutions. A prototype illustration is the growing number of residents of central and inner cities who are in marginalized situations, that is, outside most of the major institutions (e.g., the poor generally, but especially black youths from poor homes, the elderly, and mothers without husbands). But the unemployed upper-middle-class executive is just as marginalized in these days of swiftly obsolescent skills. The marginalized, whoever and wherever they are, are regarded as having no rights to participate in the multitude of decisions that give shape, texture, and meaning to the city, to life in the city, and to much of life itself, except as they may possess the voting and other limited rights of petition and plea in their constricted role of citizen.

Even not so marginalized citizens are regarded as having substantially no right to participate directly in such urban decision making. In reality, however, when people make decisions about their city residential location, their mobility, and their transportation or engage in their everyday acts of law-abiding or criminal behavior, they actually participate not only in the day-to-day governing process but also in fundamental urban development decisions. They are not recognized, nor do they generally recognize themselves, as participating in urban decision making because they have no recognized, institutionally accredited roles therein. Theirs is regarded as strictly privatized, personalized performance and not involvement in public urban affairs. Of course, the difference in range of choices of the rich and the poor in terms of such decisions as residential location and relocation, mode of transportation to work, etc. is very great.[1]

Such institutional consciousness as this denial of real involvement because it is in the institutional underworld is prototypical of modernity and not restricted to urban affairs. In regard to urban affairs, however, in recent years events have occurred characterized by true consciousness on the part of some city dwellers and a more generalized double consciousness on the part of others. Citizen movements occasionally erupt to stop an expressway from being built or end a policy of permitting high-rise construction to destroy neighborhoods. Some people may even organize a rent strike or try to occupy vacant houses. Yet it has apparently occurred to only a few people that there may be a really different alternative approach.

This approach of which we speak, that of opening institutions to each other as well as to everyday-life processes regarded as sub- or extrainstitutional, is an alternative to institutionally reformative projects designed to cope with specific institutionally defined problems (e.g., insufficient employment opportunities, too much traffic congestion, lack of sufficient low-cost houses or hospital beds or schoolrooms). It is an alternative to traditional efforts to have government more active in solving problems or to involve institutionalized private enterprise in meeting such institutionally defined needs.

The human values that could and should constitute the matrix for more partialized professional/technical concerns are usually thought to be within the aegis of a particular institution as a matter of tradition. Other matters involving human values are not thought to be within any institutional jurisdiction. Some are treated essentially as residual matters fit for the most informally organized, decentralized institutions, such as the family (if the family is not thought to be in uninstitutionalized, everyday-life space). Still others are assigned to government or government takes them on but also as residual matters, that is, matters not treated directly by any other institutions.

Governments and political systems in modernity may be sorted into two categories for purposes of this exposition. In one, the government and/or *the* party takes the leading role in determining the matrix of human values. The shape and form of the appropriate human experiences are to be decided by government and party. It is little wonder that there is a strong impulse for centralized dictation in such a situation. The government and party enter into control of the other institutions.

In the second type, we find government as a residual caretaker for the matrix of human values. Increasingly in modernity there is a major institutional interlinking in this type. In the words of Geoffrey Vickers: "Organs of authority . . . business organizations, trade unions and universities . . . [have] become more closely integrated internally and more closely associated with government, both through its own organizations and through its more prominent members, who participate increasingly in the work of public bodies."[2] But as we know, the flow of predominant influence in many countries goes from the economic institutions and their associated institutional junior partners (science, technology, education, and so forth) to government or, as in the United States, we may have a more or less integrated military/industrial/governmental megainstitution.

The institution of government finds itself in crisis throughout much of the Western world especially where this second type of government is prevalent. A major reason should be obvious. Governments of this type are looked to increasingly by people to take

120

care, somehow, of the matrix of human values that seem to be deteriorating. These human values are often made impossible to experience in the advanced urban-industrial society except in the distorted forms that are so well known. But when government tries to influence other institutions in regard to human values, it often hears the indignant declaration that such problems are beyond the institutions' legitimate scope of concern. In fact, these human problems are beyond the competence of any institution that services or provides for particular human needs rather than for total human-experiential values. Of course if a given problem can be translated, albeit illegitimately and inappropriately, into one involving a commercialized service, economic institutions or institutions taking on an economic character may take on the production and delivery of the service. If not, it may be either ignored or left to government to perform as a welfare or social or public service.

Noting that governments of this second type, just as all other major institutions, are losing their legitimate authority, Geoffrey Vickers recommends that people should be less suspicious of the authority of a democratic state. He notes that since authority is necessary, democracy may be the least bad authority of any. Conversely, he counsels that governments should try to be better caretakers of human values; governments should be active in shaping the matrix of human values more equitably and reasonably than they do at present.

Actually, Vickers's relative optimism contrasts with a not dissimilar but far more deeply pessimistic analysis of our future by Robert Heilbroner and, even more recently, by the architect–utopian writer Percival Goodman.[3] Together the books of the latter two may well become the basic general-philosophic survival manual of the seventies and beyond. They do offer advice, which may seem hard-hearted or hard-nosed, about the necessity for a type one government in a postdisaster, postindustrial society. They both propose seemingly radical (some might say reactionary) reforms in the face of the current crises.

Vickers's proposals are equally reformist of the present urban-industrial society, but it is hoped that they will be accomplished

121

before rather than after the shocks of severe system or ecological oscillations. Vickers proposes that people accept constraints, restraints, and more authority. The authority would be applied in the direction of equity while the restraints and constraints would be directed to engendering practices more respectful of the natural environment. The result could be a more restricted society with the restrictions felt as protective rather than as unjust.[4]

We term this proposal ''reform'' even if it calls for a kind of discipline known earlier only in wartime, if then. It is reform because it assumes the continuation of the kinds of closed, destructive, authoritative institutions that have produced the alienating, isolating, privatizing, and partializing conditions resulting in the losses of governmental and other institutional legitimacy. It urges governments to operate with more sensitivity, intelligence, efficiency, and force than they have in the past in most of Western Europe and North America. Without basic transformations, however, such as those contemplated by our suggestion to open institutions, we think such advice is bound to fail. Or it may and probably will move in the unhappy alternative direction of the first mentioned, centralized type one government. In fact, one of the fundamental reasons for the growing strength of the left in Europe is precisely the impression the left gives of being effective, technocratically efficient, well-organized parties that can provide good government in the way Vickers suggests. Under other national conditions, it is exactly parties on the right that have such images. Both the left and right propose stronger, more important, commanding central governments.

Another seeming alternative, which is, however, another reform, comes from the conservative side of the more important centrist American politics. With the welfare state proposed by liberals since the Depression seemingly unable to solve the nation's problems, it has been proposed that government do one of two things. Either institutionally it should try to reduce its engagements in the nation's problems or, if this is not possible, at least it should try to improve its services in both production and distribution (so-called delivery of services). Such improvement seems to have two related dimensions, one being more efficiency and the other, more choice (than now) for those citizens using the services. If not having more choice, people as citizens receiving governmentally provided goods and services (so-called public goods) should be getting what they prefer more than is usually the case. All this requires different methods of governmental provisioning, especially moving, whenever efficiency dictates, from higher, more centralized institutional loci of governmental power to lower, more decentralized ones.

Intellectuals dissatisfied with the so-called liberal welfare state, not just conservative in the usual sense, have even formed a learned society entitled the Public Choice Society. We think they are also bound to fail in regard to moving in any substantial way on any of the nation's major human problems because at bottom they do not question the problem-producing practices and beliefs that constitute the foundations of the modern institutional reality.

This group of Americans, with its efforts directed against government consolidation and bureaucracy at all levels of government, has a kind of counterpart group of French intellectuals.[5] The latter, who are known as the New Philosophers but claim no particular ideological orientation, have as their primary target the Soviet Union—not as a deviant case but as the logical outcome of a Marxist point of view. They, too, see government in its centralized form of consolidation as the major obstacle to freedom. But we must charge them as well with a flawed, partial understanding of the underlying reality. Increasingly unmanageable problems are not coming from big government qua big government nor from big one-party government as such. Freedoms may well be more endangered by a centralized one-party state than by a truly competitive multiparty state. But a ''garrison state,'' to use Lasswell's famous term, a government of command and coercion, is not the natural monopoly of a Marxist or any other ideology that calls for the leveling or unification of a hierarchical multiclass system.

Our argument, to be clear, is that formally or de facto centralized single-party governmental systems (whatever the superficially competitive forms) are increasingly likely in all modern states regardless of how left, right, or center is the ruling ideology. They are likely precisely because of the general modern acceptance of the entire range of institutional divisions that generate problems that grow larger, not smaller, with partialized and, hence, pseudo solutions. Authoritarian government is a natural outgrowth of people's sense of desperation in the face of their increasingly individualized, isolated, and divided lives and their loss of even the kinds of coping abilities of the extended families of a generation or two ago.

This need to strengthen government and/or multinational centers of decisional power is felt not only by the lowly but also by the high and mighty of the increasingly insecure ruling classes. They, too, through efforts to understand and thereby gain control over presumably complex systems, are trying to build or support the building of an apparatus that will require more continuity and constraints and more effective governmental decision making and execution than was possible in a more relaxed laissez faire, less developed institutional world. And for every Marxist group of systems scientists, there is at least a corresponding or often more avant garde group in the American government, in the World Bank, or in the Club of Rome.

Let us briefly consider this kind of approach, which at first glance appears to be a kind of polar opposite of the partialized problems–partialized solutions approach taken by the others mentioned so far. At first glance it seems to be precisely the comprehensive approach missing on the part of the public-choice advocates as well as on the part of traditional liberals who think of problems, programs, services, or needs one by one. Systems analysis starts with the opposite assumption. This assumption is that we are dealing with a complex reality or complex system that must be taken into account at the outset lest a program be developed that fails or even wrecks other programs. Because a given affects and is affected by others, it is necessary to include all such interdependent sectors in moving on any one of them.

The new systems scientists and analysts are trying to build models of these very complex modern systems (and their subsystems) and to make very complex software programs suitable for simulating such systems on high-speed data processing machines called computers.

Such efforts, however, are bound to fail. They must fail because they have not and cannot include total persons in models of a so-called complex modern institutional system. With the partialization of total persons has come not merely a fragmented understanding but also a misunderstanding of human problems. To the extent that systems scientists understand (as most do) their work to be that of trying to find, with the computer's assistance, connections and relations in increasingly complex systems, they are modeling a complexity that is not entirely real. Consequently, they deal with not quite beings and pseudoproblems rather than real human problems. Let us briefly see what happens when such a systems analysis approach is used in urban analysis and planning.

The city is regarded as a set or system of systems or subsystems. Sometimes the elements (the basic entities or components) of the model are partialized people treated, for example, in terms of their roles or positions in a functioning economy or industry. Sometimes the elements are suprapersonal industries or firms or divisions of firms. They, too, are understood in their functioning sense. Sometimes the elements are nonpersonal things, such as buildings, that also are understood as being components of or in a functioning system or subsystem.[6]

Models of functioning are derived from the presumed objectively "real" structures: roles or organizational entities. In this kind of structural-functional systems analysis, the interest of the urban planner or urban-systems analyst is never in whole persons and their problems but rather in partialized persons or in a nonhuman system of objects. Problems of loneliness, of isolation, of boredom, of apathy or alienation, of bitterness and hostility—these are outside the purview of the technocratic urban planner or urban-systems analyst.

Because the urban-systems analyst does not model persons as such, the only concern can be with people as noted in terms of partialized institutional statistics. In reference to some of aforementioned problems, people may appear statistically mentally ill or as apprehended delinquents or in whatever partialized category a given record-keeping and relevant institution may be classifying urbanites. The urban-systems analyst may actually be concerned with changing these statistics, for example, with reducing the number of people in the city who are mentally ill. And if there is some theory that unemployment produces increases in mental illness, the urban-systems analyst may simulate with the computer what probably would happen if a certain number of new jobs were created. Or the analyst might end by making such an economic-policy recommendation.

However, at the very same time, the urban-systems analyst has a deeply rooted interest in the conservation of the major institutions and in their basic structures. Both real-world data analyses and computer simulations require this kind of stability.[7] The analyst may hope for, imagine, or even anticipate various changes in the modes of operations of particular institutions or even in regard to particular structural features or characteristics. But comprehensive change, especially in the nature of the basic elements as well as in their interrelations, is something that would be counterproductive for the analyst.[8]

But are not such changes precisely the hope of such other institutions as social work or of families, regarded as informal social institutions, or of the mental hospitals? Are not such problems and prospects of central concern to the academic disciplines associated with or the specialists concerned about such institutions: social work professors, sociologists, and psychiatrists? Are not such persons precisely those having a vested interest in change, in change *in total persons* from being mentally ill to being healthy or from being apathetic to being involved? And are not even the more mundane problems of traffic as conceptualized by the more specialized urban transportation planner or engineer *problems of total persons?*

Taking the last example first, we see that problems of traffic are not treated today as problems of whole persons or of sets of whole persons. Traffic is within a domain of expertise wherein such problems must be treated in terms of specific and partialized system or subsystem processes and categories such as transportation of goods or commuting to and from work by employees, etc. The transportation specialist would never dream of tampering with basic matters of political economy or with the central contents of other major institutions in trying to solve or cope with traffic problems. At the most, limited social or personality consequences or correlates of certain kinds of traffic processes or problems might be of residual interest to some sociologists of transportation.

Similarly, the kinds of personal and interpersonal problems mentioned earlier are, indeed, assigned to partialized specialists such as psychiatrists. Psychiatrists usually make no claim to any right to inquire into and act diagnostically or therapeutically about so-called social, or economic, or—God forbid—political conditions. So, too, do professors of or professionals in social work and sociologists find themselves permitted to operate only within domains and sectors that are considered legitimately accessible by dint of their specialized training. One of the crucial implications of professional certification and institutional membership is the designation of delimited areas and matters beyond, in addition to those subject to, the presumed institutional competence of the certified.

To be sure, various personal and interpersonal problems are often assumed to be just that: personal in the sense of being the responsibility of the person and occurring in essentially separated and residual everyday-life space. It follows, then, that if the economist can help increase incomes, the sociologist can help strengthen the structure of the family or improve recreational facilities, or the urban planner can contribute to "improved" housing or neighborhood conditions or reduce traffic congestion and hazards, each specialist can thereby contribute to the alleviation, solution, or prevention of problems of whole persons and sets of persons in their nonsectorialized or not so sectorialized everyday lives. Such is the modern logic, or at least the hope, and such is the modern failure.

It is a failure, and it is bound to be a failure. The deepest, most severe problems of modern people, at least in the moderately and advanced industrial societies of East and West, are associated no longer with material or "economic" deprivations or any other institutionally distinct, partialized problem but with the disintegration of total personhood and of human communities. There are still periodic recessions or a more permanent and large unemployment problem. We contend that the latter is increasingly less manageable or solvable in traditional institutionally circumscribed terms. The dark underside of modernization, of proliferating institutional specializations and divisions and of the economic, health-care and many other historical gains in efficiency, has been precisely that of reaching and now going beyond the point of diminishing returns.

As the positive returns are exceeded by negative ones, by the intransigence of problems, we can understand that the artificially complex mosaic we have created means a loss of freedom. Total persons have gained some anonymity and, thus, freedom although, impaled as they are on the hooks of their specialized roles or serviced statuses, this freedom can be exaggerated. It is difficult to be free or to enjoy freedom when hungry. But people have also lost identity as total persons and, hence, lost the freedoms and opportunities implied in earlier times of more human, total-person community scales.

As the measure has shifted from people to institutional considerations, it has become more, not less, difficult to understand and work to lessen a host of such problems as unemployment, underemployment, and even inflation. When such problems are understood as "technical" and to be fixed by a specialized institutional remedy or even by a coordinated cross-institutional program, as they are so considered today, it is little wonder that the voice of the people is so infrequently raised and so little heard. The need now, the human need now, is to build new human communities wherein more self-consciously total persons will provide a new, simpler, and more unified measure of problems and approaches to problems to avert the paralysis or dictatorships that lie at the end of unsuccessful efforts by the systems analysts and decision makers.

Again, by "human communities" we mean to designate, without trying precisely to describe, places wherein people relate to each other as relatively total or whole persons. Total persons relate as such by experiencing the pleasures and pains that come from relating with other whole persons. A human community provides for the *possibility* of experiencing the positive human values of intimacy, creativity, and respect. Such possibilities exist even if negative human values predominate when people treat each other as people rather than as roles or statuses. People may even regard each other with enmity, but personal animosity is one large step closer to friendship than is impersonality or nonrecognition of personhood and personality.

The communities of the advanced urban-industrial society are, thus, far from human communities. Our communities are built along institutionally specialized, often professionalized lines of partialized, usually functionalized, and often spatially segregated life activities. Often they are communities in name only. They are instead associations of more or less isolated people related to each other usually in the most impersonal, partialized, functional ways.

One of the essential conditions of increased human community is more participation by persons more aware of their total personhood in more decision making. To the extent that modernity means, as it does, decision making by institutional expertise, core human problems are not incidental but are intimately related to the advance of modernity and its mighty motor of continually augmenting institutional specialization. These core problems involve personal partialization and, consequently, dehumanization, mechanization, or technicalization of personal and interpersonal relations. What we would term partialized or pseudo participation characterizes ever larger proportions of people both inside and outside their own narrow, specialized domains. To expect massive problems to be solved when masses of people are excluded from active participation today is as futile a belief as any belief in antiquity.

We may now repeat the first part of our basic thesis in the hope that its meaning is beginning to become clear:

> The continuing modern emphasis on divisions of labor and life into increasingly specialized, professionalized institutions is increasingly futile. Such developments are increasingly bad for people: they address pseudoproblems, and at the same time they add to real human problems. Such an emphasis, if continued, may result in the demoralization of whole nations and even of all of Western civilization.

The reason for the pessimism is that the major powers of the West are increasingly relying on efforts to control, guide, and steer what are to their top decision makers obviously and naturally always more complex national societies. The complexity as portrayed is mind-boggling at the level of the entire American and European bloc of nation-states, not to speak of the entire world system. Our concerns are for what is likely to happen when efforts to model such presumably complex systems and, consequently, to resolve complex problems are sensed as futile.

It is ironic that analysts of complex systems have termed the thinking of mere mortals ''counterproductive'' in the sense of more often being wrong than right, more often doing worse than chance, in deciding what to do about problems. It is ironic because while the analysts are quite correct in their claims, given the terms in which such thinking is done, the most advanced systems analysts in the most forward-looking, futuristic think tanks, with their computer simulations, are themselves engaging in equally wrong kinds of analysis. And given the extraordinary contemporary reliance on such methods and modes, when failure finally happens it may be too late to begin to open institutions.

Actually, of course, we are not pessimistic or we would not embark on this effort to say how institution opening may herald the end of the divisions of labor and life that we find have become so negative as carried forward in more recent times. Or, rather, we are at least hopeful—and ours, we think, is not hope based merely on wishful thinking. Another person who at least a few years ago was as hopeful as we and who narrowed in precisely on ''the division and specialization of labor'' in a multitude of manifestations as being the central problem of our time is the same Raymond Williams we have referred to before. Using a somewhat different but, we judge, also valid critique of Marxism, Williams rejects an extreme fatalism. He comments:

> For there is nothing now more urgent than to take the fundamental idea, the problem of overcoming the division of labour, to the tests of rigorous analysis, rigorous proposal and rigorous practice. It can be done only in new forms of cooperative effort. . . . We shall have to say what in detail can be practically done, over a vast range from regional and investment planning to a thousand processes in work, education, and community. The negative effects will continue to show themselves, in a powerful and apparently irresistible pressure.

He then lists the kinds of things Heilbroner sees as unavoidably the human fate.

However, Williams went on without pessimism: "And to see the negative effects, with whatever urgency, can be to paralyse the will. The last recess of the division of labour is the recess within ourselves, where what we want and what we believe we can do seem impassably divided. We can overcome division only by refusing to be divided. That is a personal decision but then a social action."[9] Refusing to be divided is the personal act of a total person. For it to be persuasive for others, the why and the how need to be communicated. We have spoken sufficiently, we believe, about why people who are total persons need to affirm this to themselves and others. It is time to be more specific about how institutions may be opened so that a spreading network of interpersonal practices among total persons may begin to make the human prospect more favorable throughout this one world.

How, then, do we propose that institution opening occurs? How can it at least begin before too late? And how do we claim that what we propose does not endanger standards or threaten a breakdown of the hitherto generally effective workings of our technological society (even if it be granted that there has been a dark underside to technological growth and development)? The answers to these questions will, we think, become clear if we say we think that theoretically there are three, not mutually exclusive, modes of opening institutions, of reducing or diminishing divisions of life and labor both intrainstitutionally and interinstitutionally.

We say that theoretically there are three modes, but we do not intend to suggest by that word "theoretical" that these are only mental creations. There are real-world instances of them, as we shall indicate. What are the three modes of institution opening?

The three modes of opening or de-differentiating institutions are as follows:

1. Enriching existing and constructing appropriate new language and practices at the level and scale of human experiences of total persons;

2. Equipping masses of ordinary people with various specialized professional/technical languages and practices;
3. Mapping everyday-experiential language and practices onto specialized ones while demystifying and translating the latter into the former.

To provide a better sense of what we mean by each mode we shall speak to them and offer real-world examples of each. Two or three modes may be features of a single human project of opening.

So-called street language of the urban ghetto, of black Americans, was born and enriched under conditions of slavery and then continued oppression. It is but one example of the enriched everyday language of members of a subculture. The recent period of American black mobilization saw the creation and diffusion nationally of additional language geared precisely to communicate intimately and to give emotional support and solidarity when the human experiences constituting the thrust of the movement needed strengthening. The youth movement of the late sixties and early seventies in North America and Europe witnessed the birth not only of slogans but also of words and concepts that contributed to the awareness and development of a new and for a while more human subculture.

When major sociopolitical events occur which are not merely momentary and transitory, they are likely to be accompanied and followed by (in fact, defined by) the birth of new language and new practices precisely at the level and scale of human experiences. Of course, the new language and practices may reflect or attest to sad human experiences to which people have been subjected, as in the case of the birth of the blues.

Examples of the first mode of institutional de-differentiating are to be found in the innovative Yugoslav self-management system. The concepts and emerging practices of social ownership and of self-management itself spread rapidly through the population as it became evident that important everyday-life experiences of popular participation in decision making were neither private nor quite public in the usual institutional sense of governmental ownership.

At the same time there was also the construction of new technical language, which was quickly absorbed by masses of ordinary people, the latter being a mode 2 kind of de-differentiating process. This effort included the concept of workers' councils with various associated participatory practices.

The concept of social ownership nicely illustrates that the language of everyday life often is not precise; frequently it is and must be ambiguous, often it has words of multiple and elusive meanings, and it is vaguely connotative rather than denotive. Human experiences, as integral, multifaceted moments fusing emotion and reason, are admittedly difficult to capture or to speak about even in poetry. One of the bases for the development of modern institutions, with their more specialized professional/technical languages, is precisely the presumed need for more precision in speech and operations.

Yet it is clear that not only is the cost a movement away from total persons. It is also clear or should be clear that the presumed clarity and precision proves, upon serious reflection, to coexist with language that obfuscates and mystifies rather than clarifies or enlightens. Even the most scientific of the partialized disciplines—connected as they must be to so-called natural language of so-called everyday life—are, at very crucial points, filled with ambiguities, impression, and mystery. And we should not forget, on the other side, that in the noninstitutionalized side of life, language and practices can be sometimes gratifyingly or shockingly precise.

What has happened in the development of modern specialized institutions, then, is the construction of an often spurious precision and the movement away from total, real people to partialized, abstract, unreal people. This process can be witnessed perhaps most easily in medical and health-care projects, in such fields as urban planning, and in the social sciences. But it is something that pervades all of modernity's institutions.

No matter how manifestly imprecise or inadequate is the language of everyday life, its strengthening, enrichment, and expansion within the very bowels of institutions in order to demystify and open up the latter is a highly desirable purgative or, to switch metaphors, a breath of fresh air that may help to bring to more human life the less than total people who professionally practice their technical trades.

A nearly unique program exists in the United States designed to teach masses of ghetto, disadvantaged, and presumably often stupid youngsters the supposedly abstruse, difficult technical language and manipulative operations of mathematics. Such mathematics is usually taught only at the university level to small numbers of students. The program is called Project SEED.[10] Initiated by William Johntz in Berkeley, California, SEED demonstrates in a rather incredible fashion some of the possibilities of mode 2 differentiating. If almost every young person, no matter if his or her IQ is supposed to be low, can easily learn higher mathematics when some simple and obvious conditions are met, the possibilities are much greater for this institution-opening strategy than one might think.

Examples of projects centering on mode 2 de-differentiating are not difficult to find historically, but they are usually transitory. They are transitory either because they tend to be ''emergency'' programs that end with the emergency, or else they are not understood and appreciated as institution-opening projects.

During World War II, for example, there was a governmental program in the United States to prepare a relatively large number of lay persons to serve aboard merchant ships as doctors. People trained intensively for a few months and then had an additional month or so of intensive ''internship'' in a government hospital. Such a mini–medical school course was far from ideal, and it ended with the end of the war. But it was in the spirit and practice of a mode 2 program, and it was carried out rather successfully despite a great deal of initial scepticism on the part of medical professionals involved.

There are many efforts, often in so-called adult education, wherein nonspecialists may begin to become versed in the specialist's language and domain. The most advanced example of the latter may be the Open University in Britain, or variants thereof in many other countries. But these efforts all share a characteristic that puts them outside mode 2; namely, they tend to be geared to small subsets of people who are interested in entering at a later age or in a different way than is usual a path leading to membership in an expert but exclusive institutional community.

A better example of mode 2 de-differentiating, although on a very small scale, is the development by a number of women in Toronto, Canada, of a women's health collective in the early seventies. The collective was regarded as a medical/health-care project that could succeed only to the extent that it was simultaneously a learning and a socially enriching experience. It was not merely a project in medical education.

It involved a collaborative team of professional medical persons, including a woman physician, and nonprofessional persons with whom she worked closely. They in turn worked with other women who came to the center with various manifestly medical or physical health problems. In the process, a new kind of social medicine was developing which was interpreting and handling various presumably medical problems as having a social genesis and needing more or other than medical or professional medical therapy. This project therefore necessitated both a mode 3 kind of demystification of specialized medical language and practices and a mode 2 provision of professional/technical terms for ordinary lay women to understand and use.

Other cogent examples of mode 3 inter- as well as intrainstitution opening come from the area of the law. Efforts are under way in some places to rewrite law and legal procedures so that very ordinary people can engage in legal self-practice. It is necessary both to map everyday-experiential language onto specialized languages and to demystify, to make clear and understandable, the technical abstruseness with which the law is so often replete.

An even more striking illustration is from the domain of criminal justice and the system of law enforcement institutions. It is a program in Canada first formulated in Toronto on a small scale and then introduced on a wider scale in British Columbia. It was developed by John Hogarth when he was an Osgoode law professor and afterward when he became the director of the police commission of the province of British Columbia.[11] The program con-

135

templated a radical change in the very foundations of the Western system of criminal justice.

Here is an example of a mode 3 program that probably will also generate mode 1 de-differentiating and that not only opens institutions (legal, judicial, police, social work, etc.) but also strikes at the very foundations of the concepts, language, and practices that provide the raison d'être of currently closed institutions.

As an example, the concept that a person commits a crime against "the state" or disturbs the king's or the queen's peace is rejected as a useless illusion. A crime is done against another person or persons. And there are compelling reasons not to institute a punishment procedure to avert such crimes in future or to uphold the dignity and status of the state or the crown lest such disrespect become widespread. To be sure, there is an interest in the affair that goes beyond the parties immediately involved, an interest that extends into the community. But the community consists of people, it is not a suprapersonal entity called "the state" or "the government," not even if it has its personal representatives, the officials.

This line of reasoning leads to an opening of the entire process to participation by ordinary people resident in comparatively small communities. Instead of sets of people performing the by now accepted specialized roles of arrest, adjudication, and imprisonment, processes of inquiry, dialogue, mediation, and conciliation make the old roles outdated. It is a human project that not only shakes up and changes traditional roles and practices inside the institutions of criminal justice by opening them up to each other in a transformed manner. It also opens up a hitherto closed process.

This process has been closed to masses of ordinary, not specially trained people. The lay jury system itself is under increasing attack by modernists and often is subject to exceptions with the claim that justice needs knowledge and knowledge needs technical experts not only as witnesses but as de facto judges. But with the system of criminal justice, filled as it is with specialists of all kinds, a nearly total failure, this move toward more involvement of plain people with its premises as to what the human values of criminal justice are all about is a prototype of a promising, innovative institution opening, albeit limited to criminal justice.

We make no attempt to evaluate the program herein but merely indicate that in its approach it represents something of what we speak. Our feeling is that Hogarth succeeded in developing this substantial innovation because he managed to remain vitally concerned with the human experiences of total persons caught up in the modern institutions of criminal justice. He evidenced a kind of phenomenological insistence on seeing what was really happening and not accepting the partializing modern myths no matter how authoritative they had become. He was thus able to contribute something that is of interest to people throughout the world.

The last innovative project of which we speak here also clearly illustrates mode 3 de-differentiation. It is a project in urban planning in a city by the name of Faenza. This is a city of about 50,000 people in the north central part of Italy. The heart of the project took place in the years 1975 and 1976. The project was intended to initiate a substantial degree of participatory urban planning and urban self-management.[12]

The need for a project to help maintain and revitalize the historic center of the city, which contained almost a quarter of the population, led to the creation initially of a traditional planning operation. A group of four urban planners were appointed to analyze the housing, public service, and traffic-pattern needs of the city center. But instead of doing a traditional planning operation, the planners with the acquiescence of the city government officials decided to see whether this revitalization project could be opened up to authentic participation by ordinary residents of the city. In the process of examining this possibility, the planners found that they could not use the technical, partializing, nonperson categories of professional urban planning if they wanted to involve people.

In their most personal, intimate moments peope do not live, think, or act in terms of the physicalistic norms and standards used by professional urban planners. The commercialized housing market as well as the public housing sector provided houses or apartments as such, but people as potential buyers approached them in terms of the real human experiences, good and bad, positive and negative, that concerned them when they dealt with housing. Housing, as we suggested earlier, is more than a need for shelter.

137

Houses signify human values that in turn symbolize sets of human experiences anticipated, desired, or dreaded.

Housing is ordinarily involved in many kinds of intimate daily living experiences. And housing as conceived, designed, sold, or rented in the increasingly consumer society of modern Italy was an element in the increasing isolation, privatization, and loneliness of Faentinians. Such experiences characterized the elderly and housewives—but not only them—in the city's center and suburbs more than in the still large, extended-family agricultural environs. Yet both the private housing industry and those entrusted to provide public housing stubbornly but understandably avoided going beyond housing as shelter to the matter of housing in these kinds of "social," "political," or "personal" contexts.

Risking—and receiving—the charge of being sociologists and not urban planners, the planners in Faenza made a major innovative effort with some local government officials, a few political party people, and a scattered handful of other citizens. Their effort was directed first to understanding what people's daily lives were like in this city. It became apparent that such an understanding could come only from a joint venture with people themselves. Moreover, it was an understanding for the citizens and planners alike, who were to become increasingly undifferentiated as the process developed.

A sample of some 800 people, randomly selected, became partners in the developing dialogue. There was an initial *conversational "interview,"* better understood as 800 teachers informing a small but interested and inquiring group of people about their lives in Faenza and their sense of the city. Additional meetings were then held. At these meetings serious efforts were made by the urban planners to trace the range of consequences of conventional urban plans and proposals, to map them onto everyday-life experiences, to demystify much of the jargon of urban planning. Much of the professional/technical language, when examined carefully in the Faenza project, proved to be just that: unnecessarily abstruse jargon that indeed was sometimes truly meaningless. And when it was neither abstruse nor meaningless, it referred to partialized aspects of objectified people rather than to living persons with values or to people's real problems.

Efforts were made in Faenza to break with the traditional image of an urban plan as a product, a thing, a set of maps spatially designating certain permitted and forbidden future developments. The urban plan for revitalizing the historic center of Faenza was not to be regarded as a specific program to be actualized in future. Rather, it was viewed as a set of projective projects that in the future would actively involve many people in working the projects through, in giving them form and substance. Whether the Faenza experience serves as the first step in a fundamental opening up of urban planning in Italy and elsewhere remains to be seen.

We say "first step" because we do not want to mislead the reader. In our judgment—and we were involved in that project nearly from its inception—it had only very limited success as a mode 3 kind of opening of the closed institution of urban planning. It did successfully begin to demystify urban planning or much of urban planning, but only for a relatively few people. Moreover, it also involved a mode 2 kind of de-differentiation, partly as a requisite for that mode 3 demystification and partly for the political operations necessary to the efforts at more widespread demystification. And the wider effort, too, was successful with only a limited number of people primarily, we think, because by the time the concept had matured people opposed to the opening process had organized.

We shall be more specific but in the most summary terms. The local citizens employed as interviewers in the first phase of the project considered the social research an intensive, although short, demystifying "course" in urban planning. The research was actually intended to be a first effort at inducing further citizen participation, and the interviewers became "apprentice" planners. They, in turn, would disseminate the appropriate skills first to people met in the sample survey phase and, in later meetings, to neighbors, relatives, and friends of those citizens. Groups from at least one of the four major parties were also recruited to be urban planners, and efforts were made also to actively involve in such roles officials of the local government, trade unionists, and others. By teaching them what traditional urban planning was all about (including the jargon)—a mode 2 kind of opening—and by considering with them

139

the deepening human-experiential problems of living in the urban-industrial city of Faenza, the transformation of urban planning was thus begun.

The essence of these efforts was to involve people as full colleagues in an opened and transformed urban planning process. The efforts were to be extended through the network of developing relations.

The greatest success was with the interviewers becoming colleagues in such a transforming urban planning process. The opposition came from people who had aversions to, or at least difficulties in imagining, any substantial change in their own roles. Among the professional urban planners themselves there were strong resisters, as there were among local government officials and political party bureaucrats. Some of the professional planners insisted that they were neutral technicians; participatory planning was really a matter for the politicians. The politicians insisted that the best kind of planning was the most efficient kind. Efficiency implies few and not many participants, as does the concentration of power! With a new communist/socialist local government suddenly in power, there seemed to be a possibility for even greater opening than had been anticipated. But the new administration felt that the accumulated problems of Faenza after decades of rule favoring speculative interests made it imperative to have conventional plans developed conventionally by the best experts. Those plans were then to be implemented by a local government that was beneficent but did not share power directly with citizens. Trade union officials did not want to enter into such uncharted waters, given how much they felt they had to do in their specific, partialized roles. They also shared the traditional line that their involvement in the political parties was the best way to ensure that the local government would serve their clientele's interests.

Such extreme resistance was not the case for all the local officials, planners, and leaders of all institutionally identified groups. However, the most receptive people of all proved to be the ordinary, indeed, some of the most marginalized, citizens. Given the extent of the resistance as well as the belated conceptualization of such an alternative urban planning process, actual accomplishments in Faenza were far less than might have been the case and, we hope, might be the case elsewhere in future.

It should be stressed that in presenting examples to illustrate the three modes of opening closed institutionalized human projects, our purpose was to emphasize only general perspectives, general considerations, general approaches. We have not intended to suggest either strategies or tactics for such institution opening in future, which may have little or no resemblance to these instances. Because we expect that there are myriads of ways of moving into dedifferentiating, institution-opening projects, it is impossible to venture predictions as to how, when, where, and to what extent divisions of labor and life may begin to be substantially reduced or eliminated.

We have referred to the concept of urban self-management in the Faenza project. It should be clear that we do believe in the dignity, the challenge, the pleasures, and the creativity that people can have in authentically participating in civic decision making and in all kinds of human affairs no matter how exotic or special they seem to be. This we believe is good, urgently needed, and *possible*.

To those who would diminish the importance of the joy and potency felt by Faenza's citizens, accustomed to thinking of themselves as incapable and voiceless, by saying that perhaps ordinary people can participate in something as simple as urban planning but they cannot participate in something really difficult, complex, and technical, we say this: First, before our Faenza experience we were told that plain people could not participate in something as specialized as planning. Second, we are not urging or advocating more popular participation per se or in conventional institutionally defined roles of expertise. Faenza demonstrated to our satisfaction that an institutionally partialized profession can be subject to opening and to translation of its abstruse practices into personally more holistic terms that necessarily involve subject matter and domains of competence thought to be within the authoritative scope of other institutions. In fact, the major resistance to opening urban planning in Faenza was probably due to the conventional mind set of people

141

who saw schools and factories and hospitals and political parties as properly "their" business, subject only to the traditionally limited rights of planners.

The planners had no right to inquire into or, God forbid, try to intervene in the actual internal operations of these other institutional entities. But opening urban planning meant precisely that: people concerned with their city had to ask about matters thought to be natural monopolies of school or hospital administrators, teachers or doctors, corporate owners, managers or labor union officials, party secretaries, or the city administration. What is most urgently needed, then, is more participation by people in a self-managing framework but in a context of one or more modes of institution opening. Otherwise even self-management becomes an empty and still partializing technique for gaining only greater efficiency.

It is, however, such praise for self-management, not to speak of institution-opening self-management, that conjures up the worst fears of those who believe there are severe limits to any substantial reduction in modernity's complexity. We are often asked if by ending the modern divisions of labor and life we mean doing away with brain surgery. We certainly want to do away with situations wherein people are conditioned to identify themselves essentially as brain surgeons; as technically proficient professionals whose primary—indeed, often only—human relationship to the persons whose brains they carve is that of servant to subhumans.

Let it be very clear: we do not agree that specialization, that specialized languages, operations, and practices, *require* such humanly partializing, isolating, fragmenting, and minced experiences. Specialization, whether in musical composition, advanced engineering, or nuclear physics, does not require the kinds of institutional realities and beliefs that have led to such distorting and degrading consequences in modernity. And when we say that specialization does not require for its successful workings the kinds of social differentiation and stratification associated with modern institutions, many of our own colleagues are outraged. The outrage covers gripping fears of losing employment, status, and indeed for many, basic self-identity. The deeply institutionally conscious person is not only a person civilized, as Freud suggested, by institutional channeling of the impulsive id. He or she is also a person with an institutional superego protecting in the worst of cases an ego that is essentially from and of partialized institutional realities.

Let us examine the argument advanced by the Bergers and Kellner, who use the jet pilot as the equivalent of the brain surgeon in their defense of modernity, its divisions of labor, and the consequent specialized roles and partialized persons. They pose the problem by asking whether people would really want to fly in a jet with pilots who had long hair, wore beads, and otherwise evidenced a "demodernizing consciousness."[13] They are speaking against a point of view heard often in the days of the counterculture and not yet completely dead in North America. Nor is the point of view absent in socialist countries. This view is that the modern middle class is too "up-tight," too much controlled and self-controlled, too inhibited, too much mind-only and not enough body.

A feeling, touching expressiveness was posed in the counterculture as the antidote to an overly structured, overly precise personality that was seen as the natural outcome and requirement of the maintenance of a modern, technologically oriented, programmed society. The feelings against which the Bergers and Kellner argue are not dead, as witnessed by such phenomena as the popularity of various sensitivity and meditative/contemplative movements flavored by, if not originated in, Eastern mysticism and drug taking, whether the drug be alcohol, nicotine, marijuana, tranquilizers, or antidepressant pills. But let us see exactly what it is that the Bergers and Kellner insist puts strict limits on efforts to demodernize society.

They assert that modern technological structures and processes must be operated by people with particular kinds of "structure of consciousness that are intrinsic to these processes." Alternative structures of consciousness "are disqualifying . . . [to] operate within structures of a rigidly controlled technological consciousness."[14] This means simply that operating modern technology requires people who are able to concentrate their attention. They must be able to focus their consciousness on the specific matters at hand.

Rationality must therefore always dominate and control irrational emotion. Notice how emotionality is dangerous, indeed, even potentially destructive, except in the one controlled form fit for efficient production: "The logic of the production process dictates control over free-flowing emotionality. [While] the work situation does indeed permit 'niches' for freer forms of emotionality . . . these . . . however, must always remain with the requirements of appropriate work attitudes or morale."[15] Thus, the Bergers and Kellner must and do embed their analysis in the traditional private-public dichotomy, the work–leisure time dualism, lest people become in the technological society only "mechanical robots."

The impersonality required by a good Weberian bureaucracy thus has its counterpart in the technological "imperative of anonymity."[16] Such anonymity must be enforced: "The production process therefore necessitates human engineering, that is, the technological management of social relations . . . [whose] fundamental purpose is to control unfortunate intrusions of concrete humanity into the anonymous work process."[17]

Underlying these technological managerial practices dictated by the technological imperatives of the underlying production process is the nature of that production process. Here we return in spirit to Dahl, although the words are still those of the Bergers and Kellner: "The fundamental logic of technological production, on the level of praxis and of consciousness, is one of productivity." An "assumption of maximilization [sic]" is also a feature of the cognitive style of technological production; the "logic of the production process always tends towards a maximilization of results" or "more product for less expenditure" (Dahl's rationality, efficiency, and economy). In fact, the Bergers and Kellner also agree perfectly with Karl Marx about the requirements of capitalist production processes, except that they do not seem to regard these processes as crippling to the workers involved. Finally, they repeat that the controlled and cool, technologically appropriate consciousness "appears to us to be essential or intrinsic to the process of technological production."[18]

Who really can quarrel with their assertion that for piloting an airplane (forget even about efficiently or economically) a concentrated, attentive consciousness is "essential or intrinsic to the process"? We hope the reader is aware by now that ours is not a plea for more emotion and less reason. In fact, we think the Bergers and Kellner have raised a false issue, a pseudoproblem, precisely because they have implicitly adopted the traditional dualism of mind and body, thinking and emotion, rational thought and irrational (uncontrolled, free-flowing) emotion. But have they not underlined the real dangers of any effort or any direction such as the one we are suggesting? Aren't these kinds of intervention in and interference with the constantly proliferating divisions of labor that characterize modern technological production and services likely to cause malfunctioning or even breakdown of the economic system?

We certainly agree with these authors that it tends to be the privileged of the world who argue against a technological society for the Third World. But this is not a reason for taking the position that the Third World should follow the more advanced nations in destroying whatever remains of community. The Third World need not repeat the one-sided and unnecessarily distorted kind of development of ever greater and ever more efficient economic productivity as the priority goal, the supposedly separable and central social, class, national and human value to which other values may be attached as secondary (or superstructural).

The idea that controlled structures of consciousness are "intrinsic" to technological (or any other kind) of production processes is very suspect. What does "intrinsic" or "essential" mean? How conscious is "conscious"? How structured is "structured"? How controlled *must* it be? None of these questions is answered satisfactorily or even addressed by the Bergers and Kellner. They are as unconvincing as was Jacques Ellul, who lamented rather than applauded modern technology, putting him in the camp opposite that of the Bergers and Kellner. But all shared a comparable thesis about some kind of technological "imperative" wherein efficiency bred ever more efficiency in a deterministic causal chain.[19] We do not disagree with either side that once committed, as so many people are in modernity, to a technological scenario, it is extremely difficult to get people to switch to another scenario. But saying this is a far cry from accepting the notion of imperative. And of course, such an idea takes on the character of a sacred belief as it is repeated, making it ever more difficult to change.

Although nothing we propose necessarily implies the end of jet flying, a movement away from the primacy of partialized, exclusive, specialized institutions may have consequences for jet flying. We would hope very much that it would end a situation of people being only passengers or potential passengers, with no right to participate in major decisions and projects about jet flying (or missile construction or brain surgery). None of those activities is so specialized and without important everyday-life consequences for people, however nonexpert they may be, to justify a continued commitment to oligarchy in the second half of the twentieth century. We say this even though the oligarchs are increasingly a sophisticated or at least highly trained technological elite coming from the upper reaches of a set of generically exclusive institutions.

Our central criticism of the Bergers-Kellner argument returns us to our beginning because it is a criticism of these authors taking for granted and for real the existence of a discrete value. This value is technological productivity of an institution or institutional system, namely, the economy. They make the counterpart mistake to that made by the "hippies" whom they abhor. The latter desired and thought possible a life free from the need for and exercise of influence, of power. Love, not politics, is what their vision became. But the Bergers and Kellner are equally apolitical. By this we mean that they simply do not understand that politics and technological production and even scientific research are integral to each other. It is not only a matter of making one the holy priority, as the Bergers and Kellner do with production of goods and services. It is even more a matter of their creating a pseudoproblem by reaffirming a false ontology.

When they indicate, as they do, that the technological process requires a certain rational, controlled, concentrated structure of consciousness, they misunderstand that process. They imagine that the speculative poetry of science as well as the passions of politics can be stripped from this abstracted, partialized, and wrong image of the nature of the real world of technological production and of the real people who are operating therein. In other words, interpersonal influence is an ingrained and inescapable potential in every action and is an integral aspect of every interpersonal act, including those in the human project termed "technological production." Thus, social and political relations and technological processes are not separated or separable activities in life. They are integral coordinates that make sensible the human experiences of total persons.

The Bergers and Kellner are thus people of advanced institutional consciousness. They are defenders of the modernistic faith as well as false prophets of the continuity of the institutional postindustrial society. Their sophisticated modernistic vision is as indefensible as the naïve countercultural vision is futile, and for the same reason. Both visions posit discreteness of values and practices, a set of pure or to-be-purified processes, which fortunately can never exist as such in a world of multifaceted experiential moments. Their jet pilot is a parody of a person, more an automatic pilot than a person— fortunately for jet pilots and the rest of us technically specialized persons.

One wonders how aware are the Bergers and Kellner of the anthropological literature on primitive peoples: that among some of the simplest societies very concentrated attention is apparently required for hunting or fishing.[20] These authors seem to believe that with modern production and servicing and machines geared to a fast, clocked tempo, the minds and, indeed, the bodies of people have had to become equally tightly tuned. Any major shift in work tempo or rhythm by the workers presumably would violate the *nature* of the machines, causing catastrophic collapse there. Even if this did not happen, in any event it would be impossible for people to concentrate sufficiently anymore if they engaged in more relaxed production processes.

We are not suggesting here such shifts in tempo, although they may well be advisable and certainly are possible. Rather, we are curious as to why such obviously bright intellectuals as the Bergers and Kellner make such assumptions without either evidence or plausible reasoning. Our conclusion is that very close to the surface of their minds is the same kind of fear that has struck so many philosophers, politicians, and just plain people in the past when not only divisions of labor and life but also the character of hierarchically organized institutions was questioned. Any tampering with specialized roles in an institutionalized authority system is a threat that chaos could ensue. With organizational breakdown must come rule by naked force. Such a breakdown is imagined as soon as one starts speaking of a common human condition, of all people including the experts being total persons.

Any image that suggests more satisfying human experiences than most people enjoy today conjures up the kind of free-flowing emotion that, to the Bergers and to many others, seems incompatible with the human need for self-control. This need may or may not be regarded as in the nature of people through all of human history. It is, however, understood as vital to the model of man in the midst of modern technology. Technology's logic—its mechanistic, chemical, or electronic nature—produces a need for human self-control that, if unfulfilled, must mean the disappearance of that technology. So goes the nightmare. Everyman if not everywoman, and we include ourselves, has such existential fears, however deeply repressed or unconscious. Although they can be conquered, they do exist. And their existence makes understandable otherwise inexplicable embracing of tyranny or exploitation by the dominated and exploited masses as well as adherence to the sacred beliefs of modernity by educated elites.

The reader will note that we have made almost no references to another feature of modern institutions, that is, to the kind of socio-economic-political systems in which they operate. The omission of a discussion of such matters as capitalist versus socialist control of institutions was purposeful. That there is an additional and heavy factor mitigating against the opening of modern institutions in capitalist countries we acknowledge, but the thrust of our remarks was intended to underline the fact that the modernist perspective regarding the model of a person as a set of discrete needs and corollary values to which distinct institutions naturally cater is a Marxist perspective as well.

Marx was perhaps as influential as any major figure in reinforcing the idea of a natural and progressive institutional proliferation through historic time. Marx stressed the division of labor as the essential and major contributor to the development of crippling capitalist alienation. However, he and Engels foresaw distinct sciences as the motor of the continued development of the productive forces that would set the stage for revolution and the coming into being of communism. Communism might even be described as a society with an ensemble of interconnected albeit still discrete institutions of porous boundaries, with the institution of government withering away over time in the transformation from capitalist to socialist economic institutions. The pursuit of knowledge, initially used for and by capitalists to further exploit alienated workers, would be used in another branch of science, scientific socialist analysis, by the intellectual vanguard for the correct revolutionary purposes. Such science would unlock the forces and resolve the contradictions building up in an expanding capitalism of ever more specialized, divided, and dividing institutions.

In Marx's model, people were just as rational as people are still for the capitalist economy's economists. People were the moving force in history in the sense that the more rational among them would be making the scientific contributions and converting them to the technological innovations that would, in turn, first be used by capitalists for their special purposes. In this historical process there would be a development of ever-greater productive forces and, since rationality was a widespread if not universal characteristic of human beings, there would not be major, effective opposition to such a progressive development of the potentially and finally liberating forces. People's rationality was especially evident in their understanding that economic production was to be the basis of the future free society but it was to be in the interests of all and not of the small capitalist class, as had been the case.

Among modern Marxists, one stands out as speaking rather clearly to and for much of the so-called New Left of the United States and Europe. Herbert Marcuse is important for a variety of reasons, but our interest in him here is twofold. First, he was an articulate voice in the late sixties and early seventies stressing the point Marx had made more than a century earlier, that liberation could be had only through such economic development that the vast amount of hard and dirty work could be done by machines. Moreover, this stage of history had seemingly arrived. It was no longer necessary to maintain people as "one-dimensional" when, at least in the most developed industrial societies, people could become multidimensional because of the vast amount of leisure time available for other, higher pursuits. Affection as well as Art were among these other, higher pursuits. This brings us to Marcuse's second point.

Especially with the failures by the youngsters of the left to extend or even to consolidate their gains, Marcuse began to emphasize, as a kind of holding operation or interim measure, the pursuit and practice of culture as a way to at least defend against the pervasive commercialism of the capitalist consumer society. We shall present Marcuse's position on Art because, perhaps surprisingly to readers who have heard of or even read Marcuse as a radical, his is a conservative, institutionally discrete position. Most radicals on the left are embedded in just that very conservative tradition. Marcuse on Art nicely illustrates the institutional consciousness of even unorthodox Marxists, themselves often attacked by the even more economist Marxists just as Marcuse has been.

First, and we would agree, Marcuse underlines that the aesthetic is not particular to certain objects:

> I believe that "living art," the "realization" of Art can only be the event of a qualitatively different society in which a new type of men and women, no longer the subject or object of exploitation, can develop in their life and work the vision of the suppressed *aesthetic* possibilities of men and things—aesthetic not as to the specific property of certain objects (the *object d'art*) but as forms and modes of existence corresponding to the reason and sensibility of free individuals, what Marx called "the senuous appropriation of the world."[21]

He has, however, already said things with which we disagree. Marcuse reserves the possibility of a "living art" to an entirely different kind of society, a "qualitatively different society," with new men and women, new free men and women rid of exploitation. We may excuse his hyperbole, perhaps phrased in that way for political effect. The next sentence, in fact, refers to the "realization of Art" in the process of constructing the universe of a free society, although the implication still is that this occurs *after* a revolutionary change. Moreover, even in the free society, Marcuse notes, there will be necessities: "of labor, of the fight against death and disease, of scarcity." For Marcuse, "No matter how free, society will be inflicted with necessity."[22]

This encrusted notion of necessity and freedom as opposites shapes the more important point for us, which point is Marcuse's conception of Art as distinct from everyday life. It is distinct not only under present advanced capitalist conditions: "Art is transcendent in a sense which distinguishes and divides it from any daily reality we can possibly envisage."[23] The key here is Marcuse's conception of Art, which we must examine in some detail. In specifying that Art with a capital "A" includes, for him, the visual arts plus literature and music, Marcuse indicates that Form is what distinguishes Art from everything else, Art as being "essentially (ontologically) different not only from (everyday) reality but also from such other manifestations of intellectual culture as science and philosophy."[24]

Intellectual culture and *essentially different* from other human pursuits! What is this Form of which Marcuse speaks? It is the quite traditional Form; it is "the entity [that] constitutes the unique and enduring identity of an oeuvre, and what makes a *work* into a work of *art*." An oeuvre, a work of Art, is removed, dissociated, alienated "from the given reality and . . . enter[s] into its own reality: the realm of forms" by the various aspects of Form. These aspects include the ways in which stories are told; interrelations of lines, colors, and points; and the like.

Although Art, the realm of forms, "is an historical reality," it is also transhistorical—at least since Art became a distinct institution. "In all their almost infinite diversity," Marcuse says about various historical manifestations of forms, "they are but variations of the

151

one Form which distinguishes Art from any other product of human activity.''[25] Since when? ''Ever since it [Art] became a separate branch of the social division of labour, it assumed a Form of its own, common to all arts.''[26]

Specifically setting to the side the perspectives of the artist, Marcuse suggests that this special Form, common to all arts, ''corresponded to the new function of Art in society: to provide the 'holiday,' the elevation, the break in the terrible routine of life—to present something 'higher,' deeper, perhaps 'truer,' and better, satisfying needs not satisfied in daily work and fun, and therefore pleasurable.''[27] Thus, Art occurs in the breaks of everyday life:

> Art is not [or is not supposed to be] a use value to be consumed in the course of the daily performances of men; its utility is of a transcendent kind, utility for the soul or the mind which does not enter the normal behaviour of men and does not really change it—except for precisely that short period of elevation, the cultured holiday: in church, in the museum, the concert hall, the theatre, before the monuments and ruins of the great past.[28]

And ''after the break, real life continues: business as usual.'' This theme of Art as opposed to everyday life, to daily reality, is central to Marcuse. ''Art is 'alienating.' '' Why? Because ''even the most realistic oeuvre constructs a reality of its own: its men and women, its objects, its landscapes, its music reveal what remains unsaid, unseen, unheard in everyday life.''[29] The ''structured whole'' of a work of Art is one where ''its presentation takes a specific time, before and after which is the *other* reality, daily life.'' Works of Art are works wherein the materials of and from reality undergo a process of sublimation through the creative energy of the artist such that reality is transformed, transcended by the aesthetic experience of pleasure, beauty, sublimity, and truth.

The modern contradiction between form and content, between the oppressive reality of the actual culture and its liberating potentialities, however, seems to have bred a barrier to aesthetic sublimation. Traditional aesthetic experience and Art have come to ''offend the human condition,'' hence the various efforts to integrate Art with and put it into everyday life in "living theater" and other "living art" forms. But these efforts, to Marcuse's mind, are misplaced. He finds it a terrible mistake to eliminate the distance between Art and normal life.

To the contrary, he argues with some power that instead of trying to bridge the gap between Art and reality, artists ought to enlarge and underline the distance between the oppressive realities of everyday modern life and Art. Artists ought in their works "to name the Unnameable, to confront man with the dreams he betrays and the crimes he forgets. The greater the terrible conflict between that which is and which can be, the more will the work of art be estranged from the immediacy of real life, thought and behaviour—even political thought and behaviour."[30] This is the real fulfillment of the cognitive function of Art, "which is its inherent radical, 'political' function."

We make no brief here for "living theater" or audience participation in the arts in any form. Nor do we disagree that artists may intend to be and succeed in being very effective, perhaps most effective, in their political aims by doing very artistic works of various kinds. But what we reject is precisely the thinking that takes the social division of labor, that is, the institutionalized divisions of life, as fundamental reality such that the institutionalized arts, including theater, become *the* domain for aesthetic experience. It is as separated from everyday life that the drama of Art both as an affirmative part of the established culture and as an alienated negation of that culture is played through for Marcuse as for many others who understand Art as an experientally distinct set of institutions.

For such people art institutions are not suprapersonal in the usual sense. But they are suprapersonal in the sense that the experiences are not capable of being had in ordinary daily life. Art's form corresponds to the "the social, the 'objective' historical function of Art" that takes it out of an everyday reality that has become banal when not brutal. Nor is Art's aesthetic experience conceived as integral to all human-experiential moments. For Marcuse, despite the initial quotation it seems to be an experience connected to if not contained in the work of Art itself—although experienced by the viewers, readers, or audience, rather than by the maker of the object, the artist.

We hear sympathetically Marcuse's insistence that Art is not, or is not supposed to be, a use value to be consumed. The economic language of production/consumption leaves us cold as well. But in order to keep it from being appreciated as something to be used in everyday life, as a "use value to be consumed in the course of the daily performances of men," Marcuse makes of Art too special a matter. In so doing, he uses the traditional model of the person as divisible into faculties with different experiences attached to the different faculties, perhaps a major reason he makes Art so special. Art's utility, to repeat, "is of a transcendent kind, utility for the soul or mind which does not enter the normal behaviour of men and does not really change it." A perhaps unintended consequence is to belittle other faculties and associated experiences of human beings. We think, though, that the traditional model of the person and of the divided institutionalized world in which the person lives and must live while specialization takes place leads quite naturally to such hierarchies. And it leads to a freezing of the separation of roles between men and women of culture and people of politics. Whether the former are to do their Art independently and, indeed, critically of the latter and their works, as Marcuse would hope, or whether artists would be controlled by politicians, as happens in some countries directly and in others indirectly, or whether a gulf is to grow between artists and politicians is problematic. What is sure is that Marcuse's hopes for radical change start from a very traditional conception of Art and aesthetics.

Our respective strategies for beginning radical transformations differ. We have been urging the opening of institutions and the participation therein by far more persons than usually participate. Because we have been using the word "institution" rather than "project" or "node of activity" or another less familiar term, we may have been misinterpreted. We do not believe that institutions in the modern sense exist. If they do not exist, then they need not, indeed cannot, be opened. What does need to be opened are the very exclusive, very hierarchical human projects that do exist. These

154

human projects are, in fact, very much shaped by institutional consciousness (language and practice). The arts are among these human projects. They are not the place outside everyday life that Marcuse supposes them to be.

Currently, the arts are practiced in special domains by professionals, amateurs, and spectators. Ours is a hope that both ordinary, everyday-life and extraordinary, not-so-everyday-life moments may take place in person-with-person contexts that permit the aesthetic facet to be larger and more frequent than it is for most people in most projects today. In such contexts, even concentrated, highly creative, striking, beautiful works of Art would be made, it is hoped, by more people than do so today in a manner wherein such works would be more part of the "practical" and would be more inside all kinds of everyday-life reality than is the case today. Marcuse is quite right, we believe, that to have a society of quality we must have a society without exploitation. At issue is only the matter of what that quality must, can, or should consist of.

Turning from a Marxist or neo-Marxist theorist to a version of what others claim is Marxist reality, we find that in the Soviet Union and Eastern European communist countries, the model of modernity in terms of distinct institutions still is part of fundamental Marxist doctrine. There is little evidence that the new Western European communism, even Eurocommunism: Italian-style, believes in opening modern institutions any more than do the conservative capitalist parties or their governments. The Eurocommunists, especially in Italy, offer a less corrupt, more efficient, but even more technocratic and institutional approach to problems. They do not offer a basic alternative to current divisions or hierarchical organization of labor and life.

What the Yugoslav experiment puts in sharp relief is that extraordinary changes may be made in modern institutional thinking and practice with good human-experiential consequences and without major adverse effects on narrowly defined economic production. For the most part, the Yugoslav effort to open institutions was focused within particular institutions, especially the economic institutions. It has become clear that the logic of such intrainstitution openings requires the opening of the entire array of institutions to each other. Whether there will occur the necessary debureaucratization and the transformation of still deeply embedded institutional consciousness on the part of vested interests is quite uncertain.

A leading Yugoslav economist, although in fact a person above disciplines, Branko Horvat, has nicely captured the efforts involved in his country's shift from the conventional institutional consciousness to one that was at least unconventional. There was a major transformation in at least the economic institutions and, consequently, in the ordinary assumptions, we would say illusions, about the distinctly separable institutional domains of the economic and the political, not to speak of the social. Horvat comments that the change from private ownership to "ownership [that] must be made indivisible and social [meaning that] the right to participate in decision making is derived from employment and not from ownership . . . implies a thorough overhaul of the entire legal system. Yugoslavia had to change three constitutions and several thousand laws before the legal system was adjusted to the behavioral patterns of the workers' managed enterprises."[31] And we would add only that the latter were also changing nearly continuously, making those who desired only peace and quiet long for an immediate pension.

Horvat underlines how in an alien environment, such as one of private ownership, a worker-managed firm is deviant and generates fundamental questions:

> Even well intended business partners and authorities do not know how to treat it. Does it represent a business or a political risk? What criteria should one apply? Trade unions find its position utterly ambiguous. Isn't it really an employer? Doesn't it destroy working class solidarity? After all, what is the role of a trade union in a workers' managed enterprise? Is there any?[32]

He makes the point that in addition to the suspicions even of well-intentioned persons who are accustomed to another way of doing things, there are the hostile and the majority of people, who "have their own prejudices and vested interests." The consequence, then, is the following: "And so the most trivial problems, otherwise solved automatically in the existing institutional setting, will become very complicated and will require a lot of time, energy and ingenuity on the part of workers' management bodies in order to be solved."[33]

Although Horvat properly makes the point that a single innovation in a sea of conformity will make the success of this innovation more problematic and difficult, we use his comments to make another point. What he described happened also in Yugoslavia, where in the beginning the environment was alien to the development of self-managing practices. Despite the difficulties, which were not only debilitating but also liberating, the Yugoslavs accomplished economic miracles in standard terms, during the early and most difficult postwar years.

We are not suggesting any attempt to copy the Yugoslav mode of initiating basic changes, which was one of very special circumstances including that of a single, coercive party system with a heroic, larger-than-life leader who had freed the nation from the Nazi yoke. But we are suggesting that there are lessons to be learned from this experience, including ones that involve creating fundamental uncertainties about conventional categories such as "business" or "economic" and "political" and "social" without bringing on the kind of collapse often feared or forecast in any of the orders, in any of the modes of production, in any of the major institutional enterprises until then entrusted with exclusive, hierarchical mandates to preserve specialized distinctions.

It is not well understood how the Yugoslav model of a person and of a society differs from the so-called more orthodox Marxist models. Without a great deal of theoretical, self-consciousness, or sophisticated writing, the developing practical institutions in Yugoslavia suggest that in certain basic regards, some Yugoslavs have made a major change in their thinking about the nature of persons and, consequently, about the nature of interpersonal relations. It has been said that the Yugoslavs have raised the human capability and desire for creative dignity flowing from participation in the management of human affairs to a position equal to the need for material goods and services. But the extraordinary thing is that some Yugoslavs understand that these are not discrete human needs or values, that to think of alienation as a matter of being cut off from the goods or services one produces or from ownership of the means for their production is an insufficiently narrow understanding.

As people produce, they do so as participants in the seamless web of decisions that determine production. Treating as a single category or two interpenetrating, encompassing categories within this unity what are conventionally regarded as two distinct categories, that is, supervised workers and supervisory managers, results in a logic that suggests further opening and integrating of conventionally distinct, specialized, functional roles. As the Yugoslavs developed the language and practices of self-management, they began to understand that if at the most immediate production moments each and every person in a small working group does not have a self-managing capability, then there is a break in the system. The system will not provide for authentic self-management later on or "higher up" in the larger councils and assemblies of the enterprise. They then made the appropriate revisions.

Whether such progressive inroads into conventional institutional thinking will continue in the context of encrusted institutional consciousness in nearly the whole world around them is anyone's guess. Even there many, indeed, probably most, people still do think and act in terms of the more conventional human models of discrete needs and discrete institutions to serve and satisfy them.

Some Yugoslavs insist that a "technical" hierarchical organization of supervision is inevitable even with self-management. Others regard education as being properly within manifestly educational institutions, albeit self-managed educational institutions, and not within the economy's working organizations. They would not accept the notion that production or production-governance moments could be thought of as production-governance-social-educational moments. But what we might term the Yugoslav apprehension of the falsity and human distortions of traditional models is for the most part not even vaguely entertained by other communist parties of Eastern or Western Europe. Nor is that apprehension any more evident among the socialist, social democratic, or bourgeois parties of Europe or America.

Ours, then, is a plea for arresting and reducing divisions of labor and life not by ending specialization per se but relocating it within encompassing human communities of total persons, where it should be. Ours is not a proposal for "demodernization" in the sense that the Bergers and Kellner use the term. It is not a proposal to halt or reserve science and technology or to break the machines. We can now be clear and end with three alternative possibilities that we understand people face today, all three involving basic change in the past and present trends toward a more finely divided institutionalized society.

First, modernity may continue in the same directions and, as some analysts already forecast, enter a new dark age of breakdown of at least some and perhaps all Western societies. The societal collapse may occur because the complexity, albeit artificial, gets out of hand and either is not understood or, if understood, is not manageable because nowhere is there sufficiently broad, overall authority.

Second, either to ward off the first possibility or as a response to it, a new authoritarianism may develop: a new kind of totalitarianism or an old kind in new forms. Whether Robert Heilbroner is correct that such a regime would be a "military-socialist" government we do not know. But we think that if it comes to pass it would blend a "religious orientation" and a "military discipline" in the way that he imagined. The regime is likely, we think, to be popular if not populist, embraced by masses of people whether it uses symbols and slogans of the left or right. Already certain people are talking seriously about the "structural" incapacities of democratic government—in North America as well as in the "sickest" European countries.

A more primitive division of labor might return with the first mentioned collapse. Or, if the second alternative occurred, dictatorial, centrally directed and regulated divisions of labor and life might be our next fate, following the example of Hitler's Nazi Germany or of Stalin's Soviet Union but with far more advanced computers and more sophisticated computer programmers to assist the ruling elite. It is evident that both of these major directions constitute severe threats to the continuation of increasing specialization and the ever-finer divisions of labor and life to which we have become accustomed.

Ours is an effort to suggest that there is still another, far more hopeful direction. We agree completely with Heilbroner when he suggests in his "second thoughts" that the general malaise of which he spoke lies in the industrial basis of our civilization. But it is imperative to understand how that industrial society is one of false consciousness, of a false institutional consciousness, that led to and if maintained will not allow any solution to Heilbroner's problems of population growth, nuclear dangers, and runaway industrial growth. If a change in consciousness, in understanding, in attitude and action requires or is a change in religious orientation, so be it. That there is "no substitute for state authority during the period of strain in which a redivision of wealth must be achieved within nations and among them" we prefer to keep as an open question.[34] It is probably a minor matter of mood or perhaps temperament but we think the Atlas role, one of lamenting but not being able to change things, needs to be rejected. It is at least premature.[35]

There are realistic optimists today who do not lament or make pessimistic prophecies. Despite our criticism of him for retreating to the barricades of a "high culture" holding operation until the wasteland thaws, Herbert Marcuse is one such person. He goes beyond orthodox Marxists in suggesting that there is another route to a more human, more humane society than the traditional premise, shared of course by many non-Marxists, of unleashing such productive forces that the ratio between working and leisure time changes dramatically.[36] Marcuse raised the prospect, however vague, of an interpenetration of the domains of work and of leisure; a fusion of science and technology with aesthetics, of the technical with art.[37] However, even apart from his assumption of a continued high productivity/high growth/high technology situation, which is increasingly doubtful for the future, he asserted as a presupposition a "new type of man," a person "with a different sensitivity as well as consciousness."[38] Ironically, perhaps, we face a situation wherein the ratio of traditionally conceived work time to leisure time is so reversed that totalitarian regimes may arise to decide who will work as well as how the work will be done. But we need not wait for a new type of person, for someone of different sensitivity as well as consciousness. There already are people, of all ages, at all levels of the working force, from day laborers to middle- and top-level managers to engineers, doctors, and lawyers, as well as others in non-labor-force everyday-life spaces, who are at least of double consciousness.

In other words, besides the already de-illusioned—those of true consciousness—there are large numbers of people of already un-common consciousness and increasingly unusual sensitivity. Their increasing sense of boredom, their feeling of the meaninglessness of life as currently lived, their deep and pervasive loneliness in the midst of Riesman's crowd make it likely that there is another direction modern men and women may take to avoid the shoals of coercion or the reefs of chaos. Starting with even a modicum of de-institutionalized sensitivity and a consciousness of the proper place of specialization, the heaven on earth envisaged by such people as Marcuse may begin to come to pass—if experiences begin to correspond to that developing sensibility.

The apparent limits set by the world's finite ecology are only recently understood. The work by the conservative Jay W. Forrester and his Systems Dynamics Group at MIT, as well as the sponsorship of such work and the appeals for restraint in future by the equally conservative Club of Rome, not only have led to "appeals to our collective foresight" of the kind Heilbroner thinks are useless exhortations. They have also stimulated other thinkers to engage in an effort to create "a new direction . . . that will greatly ease the otherwise inescapable adjustments," to quote Heilbroner once again.[39] In fact, some of the proposals are for the kind of human arrangements long regarded as utopian. Instead of imagining a work week of twenty or so hours becoming the rule sometime in the twenty-first century, if ever, such people as André Gorz are suggest-ing it as an imperative action now.[40] Combined with a variety of other major modifications—indeed, in Gorz's own words, an economic, social, and cultural revolution—we have an appeal for transformation precisely because the earlier belief in eternal prog-ress, spelled economic growth, is understood as no longer possible.

But Heilbroner's thesis is that no one or insufficient numbers of people or insufficient numbers of important people will listen to such pleas or plans in time. Instead it will take the shock of disasters—none, we hope, sufficiently large to end it and us all—for new directions to unfold, and these directions mean less freedom even if they are more respectful of human and physical resources than our industrial world has been. Our feeling, however, is that the calculus used for estimating such freedoms is wrong. The sense of freedom we know now is so much based on illusory boundaries around pseudopartialized institutions that the space between institutions as well as that outside them seems large when it is actually very small. Such an ether of freedom seems to be diminished or curtailed with any proposal to make persons more complete and, consequently, to strengthen, to develop, and to weave anew the texture of human communities.

It is precisely to avert the coercion of more communal, less extravagant, and less wasteful societies possible in future that we suggest opening institutions such that people may with foresight, sense, and sociability engage voluntarily in human relations more respectful of themselves, of each other, and of their worlds than in our industrial-urban society of the past.[41] Still another way to put this is to say that our hope lies in changing understanding of the nature of the world's problems and prospects, in changing their basic terms and frame of reference. We are not trying to persuade or force, through traditional politics of left, center, or right, merely shifts in major policies in the institutional terms in which such policies have long been posed (the appropriate rates of economic growth, including zero growth; full employment; improvement in quantities and/or qualities of services; clear air and pure water; etc.).

The third direction, then, and the one that we propose, is to arrest and reduce divisions of labor and life by de-differentiating and strengthening the connections between and among whole men and women, including people currently outside as well as inside the various hierarchies of specialized institutional enterprises. *Divisions* of labor and life can thereby be arrested and even reduced by the seemingly paradoxical process of letting more people participate in these specializations, but not in the closed manner of contemporary institutional understanding.

What prevents this from being a real paradox is that current specializations are thought by their practitioners to be more partialized than they possibly can be. They must be and are even now pursued not merely by specialists, as the conventional wisdom has it, but also by ordinary people. Both institutionally accredited specialists and outsiders share a false institutional consciousness. The former act as if they were not total people, and the latter accept the myth that they are indeed outsiders. The masses of people do participate in the specialties: we all do science, mathematics, education, culture, and economics and we all govern. The best direction for the future, we believe, is this one of paying as much attention to letting people in as to keeping people out and simultaneously opening projects so that more people may have creative, human-experiential moments.

If we did not see at least a few examples of institutions being opened to at least some small extent in the world, we would have little hope that this will be the direction modernity will take. [42] The present is a period that we think may determine major directions of the future. What would surprise us pleasantly but not astound us is to see, in a few years, the abolition of the divisions of labor and life—in a progressive and mature manner—capture imaginations and energies in a way that has not been known since the earlier impulse to end government and establish communism. Whether this direction will be taken first by persons of the left or of the center or outside current ideologies we have no idea, nor do we really care.

There are exciting possibilities for moving along a different road than that now forecast for so-called postindustrial society. If we take this other road, everyone will participate in the great discussions, debates, and experiments that must follow. We do not know what the names will be for the categories of human-experiential moments that people with their capability, indeed, their needs and values, for making categories and naming them are going to create as this adventure unfolds. Whether the language will come from everyday life in its noninstitutionalized or in its specialized sense or from novelists or other professional artists we do not know. Whether it will be a mixture of new constructed and so-called natural language and in what proportions is not at all clear. We know that merely

163

examining the possibility and putting it into limited practice with a few friends over the past few years has been a most rewarding and, we think, optimistic indication that not all is as bleak as some suggest.

What we do worry about is the slogan's being captured, stripped of its substance by the political right, and converted into consumer goods, services, or symbols merchandised for private profit. To avoid this real and present danger, we invite those who want to travel in this particular direction to join in the human-community–building project of opening, cross-cutting, and integrating institutions. This is a mission subversive of our own closed institutions. It may be more easily accomplished than we might think if we come to understand how beautiful and sad, dangerous and delightful life can become when we end the illusion of our being inside some and outside other institutions of a kind that really do not exist.

Epilogue

Events taking place in Italy right now, where and when these words are being written, mock the optimistic note of our concluding paragraphs. It is crucial that the anarchy that prevails here be understood, lest a proper lament become improper despair or cynicism that conceals an unforgivable continuation of the old political game of follow the leader or divide the spoils.

The increased onslaught of the Red Brigades and their associated military and paramilitary organizations of urban guerrillas in 1978 makes Italy a country without a real government, in the technical meaning of the political scientist and also in the most practical, most pedestrian sense. When the instruments of physical coercion and violence—weapons and prisons—are not a monopoly of a single identifiable government, of a set of people recognized by most others as being in control of that violence, anarchy reigns. Anarchy is a matter of more than mere physical coercion, however; it is infused by

165

such social-psychological considerations as compliance or consensus, as the words *legitimacy* or *constitutional legitimacy* in connection with government imply. Italy is no longer a "republic without government"[1]—as the title of an excellent book on Italy put it in 1973. Five years later, despite forms and appearances, Italy has no government. When the identity of the one who orchestrates, directs, and controls public order is uncertain or plural, the answer to the question "Who governs?" is "No one."

It is not often appreciated that while Italy is the first modern, industrialized nation-state to actually enter a phase of anarchy since the Second World War, it was not the first Western country so threatened. The late sixties saw the formation not merely of the counterculture but also of political organizations dedicated to smashing "the state" in several advanced industrial societies.

In the United States beginning in 1969, the Weather Underground, an organization of at least a couple of hundred people, embarked on just such a path of terrorism. A militant Black Panther party emerged, with a comparable goal even if with diverse, less terrorist, but more openly armed and self-defensive methods. Apart from the inclination of the American white working class to lash out against its proclaimed tutors and the inclination of many blacks to want into that same system they call "exploitation of the masses," it must be remembered what Nixon, his Attorney-General Mitchell, and Watergate actually represented. Law and order, safety on the streets, respect for the traditional virtues—these were the slogans the national government used to unleash its secret and not-so-secret war against these modern American revolutionaries. A relatively effective FBI collaborated with state and local police forces to destroy the Weathermen and the Panthers, without regard for too many of the niceties of a democratic society. In both cases the ineptitude of the revolutionaries hastened their own demise. De Gaulle was successful in crushing small armed revolutionary groups in France. In Germany, the better-organized Baader-Meinhof gang engaged in its first openly destructive action in Frankfurt in the same year, 1969. Their struggle is not yet ended, but they have been severely weakened.

It is in Italy, however, that at this writing (shortly after the assassination of the kidnapped Aldo Moro) that the revolutionary forces of the modern urban-industrial society are the strongest and the vitality of the traditional institutions the weakest. In our judgment democracy has died in Italy. It has died much as it did half a century earlier with the Weimar Republic in Germany. The range of institutions, including the government and the political parties, proved inadequate to meet the needs and desires of people in a changing society. Our feeling is that although our institutions are not particularly efficient—in fact, often very inefficient—we do not have a country of underdeveloped institutions, as is commonly believed. Instead we have a case of such specialized institutional development that our institutions resemble the dinosaurs of old. They have proven so inflexible that they could not be and cannot be merely reformed or renewed, as is still hoped by some and is repeated as merely a slogan by many others, especially by politicians in and out of Italy.

A similarity between the Italy of today and the German Weimar Republic of half a century ago is this. A great gulf developed between a ruling elite (and those near to and still aspiring to the traditional elite positions) and minorities with distinctly opposing views. Large numbers of ordinary citizens were no longer in agreement with the view of that privileged minority, even if they did not agree with the tactics or even the ultimate objectives of the terrorists. What were these different views of the Italian reality that constituted the gulf of which we speak for these three groups of Italian citizens?

For the advantaged minority in modern Italy, there was little or no hiatus between their everyday-life spaces and their occupational pursuit of money and power. For them Italy and, indeed, most of the Western world was divided into three parts. The first part was theirs. They knew it well; they felt comfortable in and satisfied with it. The second part they imagined as that of common people, where the major gratifications would remain those of filling an everyday-life space with consumer goods, spectator sports, commercialized culture, and refreshing holidays. Then there was the third part, divisible into two increasingly linked portions.

One portion of this distant, hazy underworld was populated by the lazy, irresponsible, shiftless, amoral, and immoral people. Such people were at first concentrated in the industrially retarded south of Italy, the Mezzogiorno. With postwar migration, southerners flooded into the cities and then the towns of the north, dramatically worsening the always present poverty problem. In the elitist view, the classic underworld of organized and semiorganized crime was connected with this part of the Italian reality. The onrush of urban problems came to be viewed as essentially due not to the actions of land or housing developers and speculators or unduly narrow-minded urban planners and other overspecialized technocrats throughout the society's institutions but to the immorality of these immigrants from another culture. In this point of view, the white-collar crime and corruption prevalent in the north among the more affluent were really not crime or corruption.

The other portion of this third part of the Italian reality was understood to be the growing number of politically immoral people, especially the youth, and not merely the youth of the traditionally left part of the working class. Persons who wanted to bring about a socialist or communist Italy were regarded by most of the ruling class as perverse and subversive of the proper order of the world. The extent to which the elite regarded so-called left solutions as dangerous was a rough index of their readiness to use fascist solutions.

The vast majority of people experienced the Italian reality in very different terms. The gap between their everyday lives and their economic institutional roles was great and growing. For large numbers of periodically or permanently unemployed people, involvement in the economy was less an active than a dependent kind of participation. The plight of pensioners and of the elderly unemployed was often as difficult as that of their counterparts in the United States. Frequently in fact, they were less able to obtain public welfare than has been true in recent years in North America. For many Italians working a second job or illegally (in "black work"), without medical insurance and social security, was the only way to survive a slow but equally inexorable inflation rate of the kind that hit the citizens of the German Weimar Republic in their time of troubles.

For large numbers of younger adults as well as older people, everyday life was becoming a kind of killing-of-time space rather than the traditional Italian joyful experience of associating intimately with friends and relatives. Permanent unemployment or under-employment faced even many university graduates, while *la dolce vita* continued to be the obvious condition of a tax-evading, bribe-giving, and bribe-accepting minority.

In addition to the aforementioned economic insecurities, which were suffered even by many of those who gained relative sinecures in the vast public corporations the minority agreed to establish in the postwar period, particularly frustrating institutional events continued to occur. A continued public concern with the quality of health care did not result in a halt to its deterioration. Housing remained inadequate. A student movement of the late sixties had dissipated without having had perceptible effects on the educational establishment. Women of all ages began to demand rights—from divorce to abortions to equality with men—that made the normal male-dominated political parties as well as many in the male clergy shudder with apprehension.

There were some common denominators among these and other such conditions as an exploitive and distorted process of industrialization, especially in the south of Italy. One was the increasingly evident corruption, indeed, decadence, of the ruling class in and out of government. A second was the obvious inability of government and the political party institutions to help alleviate or solve problems or even, indeed, to stop contributing to the problems through their interventions in other institutional domains. Through the public corporations, as but one example, the Italian state had created a public-private economy that did little or nothing to solve and often exacerbated the problems of unemployment, income, and productivity. Through traditional involvement in the university and school systems, the government seemed to constantly inflame and infect a situation that was already being mismanaged by the leaders of the more purely educational institutional establishment. A disgust with government and the political parties was growing, not among the cynical who knew how to use or hoped to become recipients of the power and profits to be had from top positions in government or in the public corporations, but among the vast majority of Italians. The immediate beneficiary of this sentiment was the Communist party.

This disgust began to spread and deepen in the context of a deeply entrenched tradition of political passivity and noninvolvement. The increasing electoral strength of the Italian Communist party led leaders of that party along with politicians from other sections of the party spectrum to remain deluded. Their delusion was that traditional turnouts of members and citizen spectators at the speeches in the piazza meant real citizen interest in or hope for beneficial changes in the political system. Of course some citizens had that hope, but many others had become conditioned to a politics of seemingly endless corruption and to a life of impotence or near impotence in the entire range of institutions in which they participated. The bulk of Italian citizens deserved the American label "The Silent Majority." Apart from compulsory voting, their engagement in national and local politics and government was just about as low as in Czechoslovakia, where a single minority party dominates government at all levels, including the municipal.[2]

We mentioned that the gulf between the ruling elite and minorities with opposing views was also a gulf between aspirants to the traditional elite positions and the latter. Among traditional elite positions we include the direction of government, obtained through the normal competitive party electoral process. We include the leaders of the Italian Communist party among the aspirants, although they obviously see the past and future reality differently from the entrenched elite.

As a Communist party, it has attributed to the domination and corruption of a ruling capitalist class the exploitation of the working class in a multitude of forms. As it developed simultaneously into a European social democratic party, it began to advocate not revolutionary class warfare but reforms through a Communist party—directed, active, efficient, honest government. Such a government would control and plan the economy more and even try to instill more honesty there. But it would not expropriate much property, and it would even cut down the size of the public corporation sector to obtain greater efficiency. Fearful of a Chile should it try to rule alone after obtaining a plurality, the Communist party even had as a major objective the formation of a reformist ruling coalition with the party of the class enemy, the Christian Democrats.

The unique solution advanced more or less seriously by the leaders of Italy's six major parties was government reform, especially regarding the improved provision of services. In this more or less consensual context, small parties developed, advocating fascist solutions on the far right and various working-class but democratic regimes on the far left.

With few votes, none of these small parties seemed a likely alternative. Groups on the far right and left began to organize for armed conquest. Their common feeling was that democratic solutions to Italian problems were pseudosolutions. The far right organized several almost successful coups d'état in the late sixties and early seventies and formed gangs of armed terrorists. The far left also moved toward armed gangs, with the best organized and most successful so far being the Red Brigades.

In the Italian conditions of today these well-organized, armed gangs of the left have arisen to challenge police and soldiers. In an urban guerrilla war, they have struck at the institutions of government, of the political parties, of the judiciary, of the prisons, of major industries and factories in the economy. They have proclaimed the need to replace a 30-year misrule by the Christian Democratic "managers of the state." An "imperialist state of the multinationals" needs to be replaced by a new regime dedicated to the welfare of the proletariat. They have succeeded in establishing "people's courts" that try, condemn, and execute "enemies of the proletariat," such as Aldo Moro. In so doing, they have made resonate major chords of fear, which, combined with the aforementioned disgust, have led to a sense of resignation, of acceptance of whatever will come, on the part of many Italians.

Law and order came to be understood as due not to an eternal or even necessarily long-term state but to the armed force at the command of sometimes very vulnerable human beings in the police and military. A fragile sense of living within a relatively safe, secure suprapersonal nest of political and governmental institutions has given way, as we suggested myths do at times of revolution or near revolution, to a very different feeling. Many Italians now feel that their fate is better secured by trying to live anonymously in their subpolitical everyday-life spaces and their wage-earning activities—if the latter do not become a battleground of the political struggle. The Red Brigades are currently determined to penetrate the contiguous political/economic/everyday-life spaces of the relatively affluent political-economic stratum to demoralize and immobilize those people through fear and terror. At the same time they threaten to end the security the masses of people feel within their everyday-life spaces by undermining or exploding the political and economic institutional supports for that system. They promise the masses of people a more effective, more just, more beneficial system if they will mobilize to support or at least not interfere with the actions of the armed revolutionaries.

Whether the occasion will be used to establish a regime of the fascist right, of the hard right, of a party coalition forming a government of national unity, or even of a successful militarized ultra-left, such as the Red Brigades, is unpredictable at the time we write this. But one of the predictable effects of events so far will be a reinforced conviction on the part of many here that the normal institutions of Western industrial democracies are unworkable. Whichever party or set of parties is successful in obtaining government power, whether electorally or through armed force, there will be an attempt to reorganize the array of institutions and put them together in a much more coordinated fashion. The aim will be to reestablish a condition wherein sufficient numbers of citizens are compliant with a traditionally socialized institutional order because the most intimate parts of their everyday life have again become at least minimally satisfying. Whether the reorganization will be by command and coercion in an openly garrison state of the left or right or through a centralized power more cloaked in traditional forms of seeming voluntarism is unknown. In any event Italy's fate for the next period, of unknown duration, is unhappily foreseeable: a government and/or party(ies) taking the leading role in determining the matrix of human values (referred to earlier as "type one"). Although there will be much talk of basic reforms, revitalization, and modernization, a liberal and reformist path cannot be taken because the forces of dissent are too widespread, the disenchantment too extreme, and the weaponry of urban violence too easily obtained.

Only a foolhardy person would have predicted the Russian revolution, its Stalinist aftermath, or, for that matter, the rise and successful consolidation of the Nazi movement, even though in the latter case there was also widespread dissent, disenchantment, and relatively easy access to weapons. We shall be foolhardy and predict here that whether the Italian state that arises from the ashes of assassinated Aldo Moro and his five bodyguards is of the extreme left or right or some combination of a center left regime, the attempted institutional reorganization will be a failure. Order of a kind may be imposed, but continued disorders are more likely. Even if every single terrorist or urban guerrilla is successfully hunted and exterminated and public order prevails in a quasi- or totally totalitarian mode, the basic troubles will not go away.

Institutions that have served well in another historical period cannot be resurrected or renovated if they are inappropriate to the new situation. In Italy a public cynicism and apathy, a learning to live more or less joyfully outside the political system, has given way to national demoralization. The urban guerrillas are not the cause; they are a tragic symptom. The prognosis can only be bleak when few leaders are willing to open their partialized institutions or to share decision-making power with ordinary people and with those from other institutional domains. A nest of dissatisfying institutional domains that strip people of or fragment their community(ies) can survive only when, due to a natural beneficence and a humanly intelligent technology, people continue to prosper at least in some limited regard. When such an era ends, as it had for a defeated Germany in the twenties and has now for Italy in the post–cheap oil epoch, the only sensible solution is to construct new human projects that attempt to extend the everyday-life world to incorporate everyone and all their more particularized pursuits.

When anarchy and public disorder prevail, as they do now in Italy and as they did in the late sixties in the United States, it is understandable that people yearn for strong government. Heilbroner believes that there is "no substitute for state authority during the period of strain." But for the accidents of Watergate, who knows what *merely strong* state authority might have led to in the American political system. We all know what state authority in the context of a dream of glory meant in Hitler's Third Reich or Stalin's Soviet Union. Italy urgently needs a stronger government, but as an interim measure. It is imperative that such strong state authority be combined, in a kind of dialectical contradiction, with a softening and a weakening of the boundaries and contours not only of the state but of every one of the institutional domains, all of which need a new, more open design.

In fact, the Italian Red Brigades as well as the so-called autonomous revolutionary groups (many of whom disapproved of the killing if not the kidnapping of Moro) have a broader vision than the usual limited political one. They see politics everywhere, pervading all institutional domains. As truly orthodox Marxists, indeed as Leninists, the Red Brigades conceive of a pervasive infiltration of every institutional and separated everyday-life space as the key point, the weak link in the armor of the class enemy. Their primary objective is to capture the political-governmental heights and then to use that institutional terrain as a place from which to bludgeon into the desired mold the array of institutional practices in order to eliminate the capitalists and establish the benevolent dictatorship of the proletariat. In other words, while seeing the economic, the ownership of property, as the fundamental Archimedes point that determines the nature of the world, they understand the political as the fulcrum of the lever that does the work of shaping and forming that world.

These revolutionaries have made the world one-dimensional or of one superdimension, a world of terror, as the hippies of the counter-culture made a one-dimensional world of love. The hippies constructed a myth that politics could be eliminated; that human affection could substitute totally for human influence. The current revolutionaries believe that politics not only cannot be eliminated but is everywhere, in every form and in every moment. Their human-experiential moments are unifaceted ones of power. In fact, for them politics is defined conventionally as the array of actions designed to influence or monopolize the armed force that distinguishes government from other institutions. Their myth has it that power is the primary, indeed the only important, force. Power over people determines all else, at least until utopia is achieved.

In fact, affection for one's fellows is permissible if carefully controlled, but affection for one's human antagonists is impossible. The enemy is not other human beings, though, but an impersonal class. And just as affection is impossible for the persons who happen to be human representatives of that class, so, too, are such sentiments as pity or a sense of morality impossible. For the Red Brigades ethics are the consequence of class and not human relations, as Lenin had said. As a member of an oppressed class one has an ethical duty to kill class enemies, from the high and mighty to very humble people performing tasks for the class whose power needs to be taken and who needs to be destroyed. Aldo Moro's assassination was acclaimed by captured leaders of the Red Brigades, awaiting trial for other crimes, as an act of the highest ethics! In practice, then, the utopia of the ultra-left revolutionaries in modern Italy is for a very long and bloody time to be one of using force to take over the institutional array, not to transform it but to operate substantially the same institutions, minus those of private property, in the interests of a working-class mass rather than a capitalist elite.

What we have said about the political approach and perspectives of the Red Brigades is true, we believe, even if later on the story is revealed as more complex. It is possible that behind or connected with the Red Brigades are important far right figures from inside the political-economic elite of Italy or elsewhere; from the Italian secret services, which had been involved in the unsuccessful fascist coups d'état; from the United States CIA, the Russian KGB, Third World terrorist groups, or clandestine secret services—or from any combination thereof. The fact that major powers and groups in the world may have actively assisted the Red Brigades does not contradict anything we have said so far about their political approach or perspectives.

Their conventional albeit extreme and modernized political approach has met with an equally conventional political response in such a way as almost to guarantee an avoidance of concern with transformations or even basic reforms of other institutions. It is a contradiction in terms to believe, as do those on the far hard left, that institutions can become humane by subjecting them to the iron grip of an elitist group. It is equally impossible to imagine those of the center or humanist left opening institutions when their objective is to secure compliant citizens, affiliated party members, supportive voters, or merely clients. A lack of imagination of alternatives to institutional reforms of the usual kind by all Italian political parties makes them irrelevant in the present crisis.

Lest the American or Canadian reader think that these Italian events have nothing to do with his or her future, we need only point out that the political historian Walter Dean Burnham has aptly termed the American system of politics "nonrule":

> American politics in its normal state is the negation of the public order itself, as that term is understood in politically developed nations. . . . We do not have political parties in the contemporary sense of that term as understood elsewhere in the Western world; we have antiparties instead. Power centrifuges rather than power concentrators, they have been immensely important not as vehicles of social transformation but for its prevention through political means.[3]

The reader will understand that if one amends this quotation slightly to suggest that both American and Canadian political parties, especially those in power, share with such European parties as the still dominant Christian Democratic party of Italy the usually successful task of ordering social reforms to fit the interests of the dominant socioeconomic groups, the North American party systems are quite like the Italian system. Burnham argues, we think persuasively, that the political parties in America are increasingly irrelevant in the unfolding crises of social change—just as the Italian political parties are increasingly irrelevant.

We are not suggesting that red, black, or other political terrorist brigades of an Italian or European genre will arise in North America in a more serious fashion than they have in past. Nor would we rule out that possibility, given the increasingly multinational spread of the style and content of formerly nationally bound events. But certainly the already increasingly numerous terrorist groups and gangs in tiny Hamilton, Ontario, Canada, and in gigantic New York City suggest

176

that the crisis of institutions in modern industrial societies extends to and through the vast North American continent. It is no longer possible there or in Italy to absorb pressures or solve problems by looking to the usual prospect of economic growth with full or nearly full employment.

In Italy the shocking methods of the elitist Red Brigades, who want to be the vanguard of the proletariat, or of their fascist rivals, who defend the bourgeoisie, may jar the current ruling stratum or their younger successors into experimenting substantially with innovations that deserve that name. But it is unlikely—at least for a longer period ahead. Whether other nations take advantage of the Italian tragedy to avoid their own is also unlikely if we read history probabilistically. Fortunately for the human race and human history, however, the improbable has come to pass so often that we have no excuse not to try. It is far better to be a person ostracized by one's institutionally identified fellows than a murdering terrorist or a subordinated subject living in fear of the next wave of violence.

Notes

Chapter 1

1. See the historical treatment by Sebastian de Grazia, *Of Time, Work and Leisure* (Garden City, N.Y.: Doubleday Anchor, 1964).
2. We do not intend to restrict this statement to Marxists.
3. Werner Heisenberg, *Physics and Philosophy* (New York: Harper Torchbooks, 1962), pp. 79, 81.
4. de Grazia, op. cit., p. 29.
5. We treat Marx's institutional views at greater length in Chapter 3. That this notion of basic and less basic needs of human beings is widespread can be appreciated by seeing how otherwise ideologically divergent protagonists agree on this model of man. On the one side are liberals and conservatives among capitalist ideologues. On the other side are such widely divergent Marxists as Ernest Mandel (who opposes the idea that work can be humanized) and Branko Horvat, the Yugoslav theoretician (who takes the opposite position). All agree that a person is divisible into at least two parts, one more fundamental than the other. See, e.g., Ernest Mandel, *Marxist Economic Theory* (London: Merlin Press, Book Club Edition, 1968), pp. 660 ff.; Branko Horvat, *Towards a Theory of Planned Economy* (Belgrade: Yugoslav Institute of Economic Research, 1964), chap. 11, and his current book in progress, especially *17. Paths of Transition* (mimeographed, Dubrovnik Conference on Self-Management, 1977).

6. Frederick Engels, "Speech at the Graveside of Karl Marx," in *Karl Marx and Frederick Engels: Selected Works* (New York: International Publishers, 1968), p. 435.

7. See the comments by Engels on the importance, although secondary, of so-called superstructural elements, in letters to Schmidt and to Bloch in *Karl Marx and Frederick Engels, Selected Correspondence* (Moscow: Progress Publishers Edition, 1955), pp. 415–416, 417–418. For a recent revival of the conventional debate, see Raymond Williams, "Base and Superstructure in Marxist Cultural Theory," *New Left Review* (November–December 1973), pp. 3–16; and Terry Eagleton, "Criticism and Politics: The Work of Raymond Williams," *New Left Review* (January–February 1976), pp. 3–23.

8. In a somewhat different context the point we are making is put nicely by Russell L. Ackoff, "Beyond Problem Solving," *General Systems,* Yearbook of the Society for General Systems Research, vol. XIX, 1974, pp. 237–239 (2023 G Street, N.W., Washington, D.C.).

9. This starts, and in a sense our whole book is about, an examination of the major explicit and implicit foundations of, reasons for, and possible alternatives to entrenched institutional thinking and practices of the kind criticized so forcefully by Ivan Illich. See, for example, his *Deschooling Society* (New York: Perennial Library, Harper & Row, 1970). In this particular regard, Illich proposes a "convivial" society in contradistinction to one of long-standing "industrial productivity." We find his intention good, but such a proposal must be only a first, most general step in the forging of a new understanding that would include, we would argue, an interpenetration of conviviality and many kinds of productivity, including industrial. See his *Tools for Conviviality* (New York: Harper & Row, 1973), p. 11.

10. The author is deeply indebted to Benjamin N. Agger of Waterloo University in Canada for formulating this conception of the primal human moment, which I have borrowed almost literally. It was perhaps the last, key insight that allowed me to move from my own institutional thinking and practical professional practice as a political scientist to whatever else it is I do now.

Chapter 2

1. This point is made eloquently by C. West Churchman in his *Challenge to Reason* (New York: McGraw-Hill, 1968).

2. This kind of need-value identity is clear in the work of many psychologists, but the ideas of Abraham H. Maslow have been particularly influential for those persons impressed with the concept of a natural hierarchy of human needs. See his "A Theory of Human Motivation," *Psychological Review,* Vol. 50 (1943); *Motivation and Personality* (New York: Harper & Row, 1954); and *Toward a Psychology of Being* (Princeton, N.J.: Van Nostrand, 1962).

3. See, for example, Herbert A. Simon, *Models of Man* (New York: Wiley, 1957), especially chap. 15, "Rational Choice and the Structure of the Environment," pp. 261–273.

4. Robert A. Dahl, *After the Revolution?* (New Haven: Yale University Press, 1970), pp. 42–44. For a fair assessment of the *corpus* of Dahl's work see George Von der Muhll, "Robert A. Dahl and the Study of Contemporary Democracy," *The American Political Science Review,* vol. LXXXI, no. 3 (September 1977), pp. 1070–1096.

5. Dahl, op. cit., pp. 41–42.

6. Karl Marx and Frederick Engels, *The German Ideology*, edited by C. J. Arthur (New York: International Publishers, 1970), pp. 50–51.
7. Ibid., p. 51.
8. See Karl Marx, *Capital, Volume I*, edited by Frederick Engels (Moscow: Foreign Languages Publishing House), chap. I, sec. 4, "The Fetishism of Commodities and the Secret Thereof," pp. 71–83.
9. See Simona Ganassi Agger, *Urban Self-Management* (White Plains, N.Y.: M. E. Sharpe, 1978).
10. Karl Marx, *The Grundrisse*, translated by Martin Nicolaus (London: Penguin Books, 1973), p. 91. We say "middle-aged" to avoid the comment that such thoughts could have come only from the young, immature Marx, who was supposedly very different and either more or less correct than the more mature Marx. We think that one relatively constant Marx is the more accurate image.
11. Loc. cit.
12. Ibid., p. 92.

Chapter 3

1. Despite efforts by economists in such specialties as welfare economics or utility theory, they have not been successful in finding a substitute for monetary values as the indicator of use values. Perhaps the most famous modern exception is the late E. F. Schumacher, who starts, does, and finishes his economic analysis with use values and even has total persons rather than partialized economic individuals as his basic unit of concern. See his *Small Is Beautiful* (New York: Harper & Row, 1973). See also his "Technology for Everybody," an address given by Schumacher at the appropriate technology conference, "Live from the Midwest," in March 1977, since published in the magazine *Doing It: Humanizing City Life,* no. 7, July 1977, pp. 14–18 (P.O. Box 303, Worthington, Ohio 45085).
2. There are, of course, various intellectual currents concerned with the right-hand side of the diagram. Among the most notable in social psychology is the work of Tolman on purposive behavior, to which Krech and Crutchfield attribute priority in distinguishing "molar" from "molecular" units of behavior. See their own molar approach, one embedded in a psychological tension initiation–tension reduction kind of frame, in David Krech and Richard S. Crutchfield, *Theory and Problems of Social Psychology* (New York: McGraw-Hill, 1948), pp. 30 ff. In counterpoint, at the left-hand side in psychology is B. F. Skinner; see his *Beyond Freedom and Dignity* (New York: Knopf, 1971) or see Richard de Charms'comments on Skinner in comparison with other psychologists whose approach is more toward the center or right of the diagram, in his *Personal Causation* (New York: Academic Press, 1968).

   Someone who is even more difficult to identify by academic specialization and whose approach we find especially compatible and fruitful is John Seeley. See, for example, his *The Americanization of the Unconscious* (New York: International Science Press, 1967) and his "Thirty Nine Articles" in *The Critical Spirit,* edited by K. Wolff and B. Moore, Jr. (Boston: Beacon Press, 1967). See also, for another example, Alexander H. Leighton, *My Name Is Legion: Foundation for a Theory of Man in Relation to Culture*, Volume I of the Stirling County Study of Psychiatric Disorder and Sociocultural Environment (New York: Basic Books, 1959).

   All such efforts represent preliminary gropings toward an understanding of the appropriate concepts, categories, and terms, an understanding that probably will be expressed more often in the richer language of poets or of some novelists than in the language of social psychologists or social scientists of any kind. Any such expression may be more widely diffused among ordinary people or, to put the matter in slightly different words, people may participate more in poetry or in more adequate and richer poetry in an encompassing everyday life than they have in past.

3. Letter from Sherrill E. Edwards, president, The Chairman Corp., Dallas, *Fortune*, December 1977, p. 46.
4. Williams, op. cit.
5. Ibid., p. 15.
6. Loc. cit.
7. Ibid., p. 16.
8. Harold D. Lasswell and Abraham Kaplan, *Power and Society* (New Haven: Yale University Press, 1950), p. 25.
9. Despite the occasional accounts to the contrary even by scientists or mathematicians describing the purposeless play in which they sometimes engage *in their work,* ours is a modernity of deadly earnestness. Playing is nearly the same crime against the state or the economy in Soviet and American factories or offices.
10. Herbert Marcuse, *One-Dimensional Man* (Boston: Beacon Press, 1964).
11. It would be interesting to see theorists of personality move on the matter of maturity in this manner. It is quite coherent with the Tavistock school of so-called existential psychology. David G. Cooper has conceptualized the onset of madness as one's beginning to understand and acknowledge a reality not seen—yet—by one's fellows. In this sense the great scientists were mad and, indeed, they were sometimes so treated by their colleagues. We understand that many people may regard what we think is false institutional consciousness to be true reality and may feel we are mad, if not merely mistaken, and certainly immature. See Cooper's *Death of the Family* (London: Penguin, 1971).
12. Readers familiar with the centrality of the concept of values in the social sciences generally and in political science especially may be interested in considering how Lasswell and Kaplan treat the concept. We cite them because they have been more self-conscious and penetrating than so many others whose fame has come closely connected to their use of the values concept in their own work. Lasswell and Kaplan portray all institutions (in a non-suprapersonal manner) as patterns of cultural traits specialized to the shaping and distribution of a particular value or set of values. Cultural traits are merely acts characteristic of groups of people. Acts are practices when "characterized according to the kind of operation and the perspectives in which it is performed."

Thus, the stuff of institutions is specialized practices, value-specific practices, special language–impregnated practices. To Lasswell and Kaplan institutions, with their defining practices, are based on distinguishable values, that is, on desired events. In fact, they offer examples of values, of desired events, without a precise definition of the term. It is one of their primitives. But their examples suggest that for them values crosscut institutional conceptions. Power as a value, for example, is not restricted to institutions of government.

In contrast, for most people, scholars as well as lay persons, when values are not taken simply as identical with, equivalent to, or a direct outgrowth of needs, they are assumed to be understandable and communicable in contemporary institutional language. There is a commonsensical, seemingly true quality to the root institutional-value categories that we are questioning: the economic, the artistic, the religious, etc. It is precisely for this reason that the portion of our diagram indicating the domain of human community, of everyday life, is not easily filled in with noninstitutional words of widely shared meanings. Values have for the most part been framed and phrased in terms of partialized desired events, that is, in institutionally partialized and institutionally specific terms. It is understandable that desired events and, indeed, undesired ones should have come to be described in the institutional languages of a society.

13. Marx and Engels, *The German Ideology,* pp. 42–51.
14. Ibid., pp. 46–47.
15. Ibid., p. 83; Marx, *The Grundrisse*, p. 163.
16. Marx and Engels, *The German Ideology,* p. 53.
17. Loc. cit.
18. Loc. cit.
19. Ibid., p. 55.
20. Ibid., p. 82.
21. Ibid., pp. 83–84.
22. Marx, *Capital, Volume I*, p. 72.
23. Marx, *The Grundrisse*, p. 163.
24. Marx, *Capital, Volume I*, p. 368.
25. Marx, *The Grundrisse*, pp. 692–693.
26. Marx, *Capital, Volume I*, p. 488.
27. Marx, *The Grundrisse*, p. 712.
28. Loc. cit.
29. Marx, *Capital, Volume I*, p. 488.
30. Marx and Engels, *The German Ideology,* p. 47.
31. Ibid., p. 50.
32. Ibid., pp. 46–47.
33. Loc. cit.
34. Ibid., p. 57.
35. Loc. cit.
36. Ibid., p. 58.
37. Ibid., p. 46.
38. Marx, *The Grundrisse,* p. 100.
39. Ibid., p. 101.

Chapter 4

1. Although he seems to accept without question institutional conceptions of values, Herbert A. Simon does not offer an institutional conception of ''power.'' See his ''Notes on the Observation and Measurement of Political Power,'' *The Journal of Politics,* vol. 15 (1953), pp. 500–516. He uses Lasswell and Kaplan's concept of influence and identifies influence with power. The two are conceptually and definitionally distinguished in Robert E. Agger et al., *The Rulers and the Ruled* (Belmont, Calif.: Duxbury Press, 1973), abridged. In the latter, however, as in Simon's conception, there is implied a process of influence that can be thought about or treated, analytically at least, as unidimensional, as single-valued.
2. Such a viewpoint is implicit throughout Sheldon S. Wolin's *Politics and Vision* (Boston: Little, Brown, 1960). Because political institutions are central to Wolin, as to most other political scientists, his is a classic institutional conception, involving, in fact, the making a reality of the institution itself, not merely the officials of the institution. In fact, this book is essentially a critique of modern social scientists for seeing politics everywhere and not only in the institutions of government (and of

politics, properly speaking). Wolin speaks of people operating the political institutions, the central distinguishing function of politics being the "relation function" performed by political institutions, and he frequently speaks of these institutions as "they" or "them" despite or perhaps because of his conception of practices as being institutionalized processes (and political practices as involving the public part of the private-public dichotomy). Op. cit., pp. 6–7.

3. Williams, op. cit., p. 13.

4. Marx, *The Grundrisse,* p. 497.

5. Maxine Sheets, *The Phenomenology of Dance* (Madison: The University of Wisconsin Press, 1966), p. 10.

6. Marx and Engels, *The German Ideology,* p. 109.

7. Such so-called structural analysis is the heart of most American sociology and of many major bodies of Marxist analysis. It is also central to much of economics, and both political scientists and psychologists spend a good deal of time inside such paradigms searching for structural mechanisms, structural change, and the like. This is not the place for a thorough demystifying reconsideration of that ontological and/or epistemological concept of structure, but it is needed.

8. The term "everyday life" is associated with several modern intellectual streams of thought. It is associated particularly with the work of Alfred Schutz and his successors, who from the 1930s on became concerned with the social-life world from a phenomenological perspective. It is also associated with the works of Henri Lefebvre, a French philosopher-sociologist of a contemporary and rather distinctive Marxist stamp. Since World War II he has published such major works on or intimately concerned with the concept of everyday life as his three-volume *Critique de la vie quotidienne,* his *La Révolution urbaine,* and his *La Vie quotidienne dans le monde moderne.* We refer to the English translation of the last in note 9. Everyday life is a central concept in a stream of American sociology of an anthropological fieldwork character termed "ethno-methodology." As the reader will understand, our usage is nearly but not quite the same as Lefebvre's, and in fact we think it is not incompatible with the implications of the other approaches or perspectives.

9. Henri Lefebvre, *Everyday Life in the Modern World* (New York: Harper Torchbooks, 1971), pp. 15–16.

10. Ibid., p. 12.

11. Ibid., p. 26.

12. Ibid., pp. 24–25.

13. Ibid., p. 25.

14. Ibid., pp. 30–31.

15. Ibid., p. 31.

16. Ernest Nagel, *The Structure of Science* (New York: Harcourt, Brace, 1961), pp. 2, 12.

17. Ibid., pp. 12–13.

18. Ibid., p. 2.

19. Ibid., p. 12.

20. Ibid., p. 12.

21. See Maurice Natanson, *The Journeying Self* (Reading, Mass.: Addison-Wesley, 1970). Although we are critical here of a tendency by phenomenologists to separate common-sense knowledge of the world from not-so-common-sense constructs, our argument about institutions might itself be regarded as properly phenomenological and in the spirit of what Alfred Schutz urged social theorists to do. See, for example, Schutz's *Phenomenology of the Social World,* translated by G. Walsh and F. Lehnert (Evanston, Ill.: Northwestern University Press, 1967); his "Common-sense and Scientific Interpretation

of Human Action," *Philosophy and Phenomenological Research,* Vol. 14 (September 1953), pp. 1–37; and his "Concept and Theory Formation in the Social Sciences," in *Philosophy of the Social Sciences,* edited by M. Natanson (New York: Random House, 1963), pp. 231–249.

22. Ibid., p.1.
23. Ibid., p. 122.
24. Sheets, op. cit., p. 46.
25. Ibid., p. 43.
26. Ibid., p. 44.
27. See the discussion on these points in Heisenberg, op. cit.
28. Lasswell and Kaplan, op. cit., p. 184.
29. Loc. cit.
30. We speak essentially of *One Flew over the Cuckoo's Nest,* Kesey's magnum opus, and the larger set of masterpieces of Kafka.
31. Although addressed primarily to the Third World, we find Paulo Freire's work most congenial and spiritually close to ours. See his *Pedagogy of the Oppressed* (New York: The Seabury Press, 1970). We find also the work of John McKnight most important. He is associate director, Center for Urban Affairs, Northwestern University, Evanston, Illinois. He is engaged precisely in projects to open institutions in our terms. Illich refers to him in the preface to Illich's *Medical Nemesis* in the following manner: "My thinking on medical institutions was shaped over several years in periodic conversations with John McKnight and Roslyn Lindheim. McKnight is now working on a book which deals with the political process by which service institutions can be made innocuous without depriving society of their continued existence." (London: Marion Boyars, 1975, p. 9.)

Chapter 5

1. See Simona Ganassi Agger, op. cit.; and David Harvey, *Social Justice and the City* (London: Arnold, 1975).
2. Geoffrey Vickers, *Freedom in a Rocking Boat* (London: Penguin Books, 1972), pp. 186–187.
3. See Robert Heilbroner, *An Inquiry into the Human Prospect* (New York: Norton, 1975); and Percival Goodman, *The Double E* (Garden City, N.Y.: Doubleday Anchor, 1977).
4. See Geoffrey Vickers, "Making Institutions Work," *Architectural Design (AD),* Vol. XLVI (February 1976), pp. 81–83.
5. For a simple, clear statement of this American position, see Robert L. Bish and Vincent Ostrom, *Understanding Urban Government: Metropolitan Reform Reconsidered* (Washington, D.C.: American Enterprise Institute for Public Policy Research, 1973), especially Chap. 3, "The Public Choice Approach," pp. 17–34. For the French view see Bernard Henri-Lévy, *La Barbarie à visage humain* (Paris: Grasset, 1977) and André Glucksmann, *Les Maîtres pensants* (Paris: Grasset, 1977).
6. Perhaps the classic urban-systems analysis and one that fits this description is Jay Forrester, *Urban Dynamics* (Cambridge, Mass.: MIT Press, 1970).
7. A very clear, informative, and less technically written book than Forrester's illustrates the conservative bias of urban-systems analysts, who feel compelled to or desire to think in terms of doing things within the kind of institutional systems and subsystems that already exist is J. E. Gibson, *Designing the New City: A Systematic Approach* (New York: Wiley, 1977).

8. A notable exception is the systems scientist Stafford Beer. He underlines the point—and the problem—of treating as the basic entities of a human system people who are not actually fixed entities. See his *Designing Freedom* (Toronto, Canada: Canadian Broadcasting Corp., 1974). He mentions therein his work for Allende in Chile. There he started to open systems operations, including the use of computers, to masses of nonspecialized persons. For a longer description of this effort see his *Platform for Change* (New York: Wiley, 1974).

9. Raymond Williams, *The Country and the City* (London: Palladin, 1975), pp. 367–368.

10. The descriptive materials and outside evaluations can be obtained from Project SEED, Inc., 2336-A McKinley Ave., Berkeley, Calif. 94703.

11. It is described in John Hogarth, "Alternatives to the Adversary System," revised copy (October-November, 1973, mimeographed).

12. For a more extended description see Simona Ganassi Agger, op. cit., chap. V.

13. Peter Berger, Brigitte Berger, and Hansfried Kellner, *The Homeless Mind* (New York: Vintage Books, 1974), pp. 217–218.

14. Loc. cit.

15. Ibid., p. 35.

16. Ibid., p. 32.

17. Loc. cit.

18. Ibid., p. 39.

19. See Jacques Ellul, *The Technological Society* (New York: Knopf, 1964).

20. For a most relevant discussion of primitive people, their way of thinking, and their practices, see Stanley Diamond, *In Search of the Primitive* (New Brunswick, N.J.: Transaction Books, 1974).

21. Herbert Marcuse, "Art as Form of Reality," *New Left Review*, No.74 (July–August 1972), p. 57.

22. Ibid., p. 58.

23. Loc. cit.

24. Ibid., p. 52.

25. Ibid., p. 53.

26. Loc. cit.

27. Loc. cit.

28. Loc. cit.

29. Ibid., p. 54.

30. Ibid., p. 57.

31. Branko Horvat, "Why Are Inefficiencies of Private Enterprises Tolerated?" *Economic Analysis and Workers' Management*, vol. IX, no. 3–4 (Beograd, 1975), p. 344. Horvat makes the point that the inefficiencies of a learning period and the increased costs of a participatory organization are more than made up for by a reduction in the often unappreciated inefficiencies of a traditional hierarchical organization. To see this point, to appreciate the concern that Yugoslav economists have for such matters as efficiencies, and to moderate the fears of those who anticipate collapse of entire systems with any basic changes, see his article, "Workers' Management," *Economic Analysis and Workers' Management*, vol. X, no. 3–4 (Beograd, 1976), pp. 197–214.

   Horvat's comment that "I came to the conclusion that the inherited authoritarian attitudes are so deeply ingrained that they are unconsciously carried into self-management," based on his own experience, is evidence for us that (1) what we term "institutional consciousness" has aspects that make the problem of its transformation very difficult but that (2) it is possible to recognize and cope with such deep difficulties as the Yugoslavs have done and remain optimistic. Ibid., pp. 209–210. An American economist, Jaroslav Vanek, has argued the case for a labor-managed market economy being more efficient than the more conventional economy to which we are accustomed. In a book addressed to a less specialized audience, he has used Yugoslavia as an example of the direction he believes the world must move to attain a state of equilibrium assuming that "the members of that society cannot be divorced from the political and economic decision-making processes affecting them." See his *The Participatory Economy* (Ithaca, N.Y.: Cornell University Press, 1974), p. 54. Both Horvat and Vanek, we believe, share the spirit of our approach, although we do not suggest that either would agree with our particular premises or argument.

32. Marcuse, op. cit., p. 57.
33. Ibid.
34. Heilbroner, op. cit., pp. 160–161.
35. For a more optimistic essay on the future, wherein he comments that many Americans have been behaving as if their country's situation was "hopeless but not serious," see Christian Bay, "From Contract to Community: Thoughts on Postindustrial Society," in *From Contract to Community: Political Theory at the Crossroads,* edited by Fred R. Dallmayr (New York: Marvel Dekker, 1978).
36. Marxists naturally suggest that only under socialism is it possible to have such a flowering of productive forces that necessary labor time can be reduced to a minimum. Often Orthodox Marxists are opposed to the positions of other Marxists, such as so-called socialist humanists, e.g., Erich Fromm, and to the entire concept of worker self-management because the former believe it is necessary to eliminate or reduce to a minimum "necessary" work time. See, for example, Ernest Mandel, *The Formation of the Economic Thought of Karl Marx* (New York: Monthly Review Press, 1971), Chap. 7, "The Grundrisse, or the Dialectics of Labor Time and Free Time." For a perspective with which we agree, see Gad Horowitz, "Human Nature and Human Community: One Man's Technical Apparatus Is Another Man's Forest," in A Report on the International Meeting on Urbanism, Human Community and Self-Management, 2508 Dorsoduro, Venice, Italy 30125, pp. 5–9.
37. See his *An Essay on Liberation* (Boston: Beacon Press, 1969), chap. I, "A Biological Foundation for Socialism."
38. Ibid., p. 21.
39. Heilbroner, op. cit., p. 134.
40. From an interview with Gorz about his latest book, *Ecologie et politique,* published in the Italian magazine *Panorama* (January 31, 1978), pp. 97–104.
41. Despite his use of familiar institutional categories (economic) as well as a theory about human needs that we have been criticizing, Branko Horvat's sensitive, searching, and persuasive treatment of how we may move from our present unpleasant prospect to one in which people are capable of coping with much more precarious ecological systems than ever imagined previously should be examined with attention by every seriously concerned person. See his piece on "paths of transition" in *Economic Analysis and Workers' Management,* vol. XI, no. 3-4 (Beograd, 1977).
42. Although we have made no effort to inventory these happenings in this book, we cannot resist a last example, which, as it happens, was the opening of an educational institution beginning some time before Illich wrote his *Deschooling Society.* The example is the work started by John Herriott in redesigning schools, founded on the premise that all persons, including so-called students, are total persons, are themselves total structures or systems and not merely or at all fixed entities within systems. See, for example, his unpublished paper, "Individualization" (Toronto: The Ontario Institute for Studies in Education, Bloor St.), or the actual innovations carried out in selected Ontario school systems.

A final note for people who happen themselves to be working in academic institutions is this. If they want to participate in opening their own institution or help to open "other" institutions, they need to be aware that they can probably expect much resistance from their own colleagues and "superiors" because theirs is not an institutionally authorized role. They may have to be subtle! A useful report in point describes a properly positioned effort at "applied research" by people in the Work Research Institute in Oslo. The amount of time required (in years!) is clearly specified, as is the need to avoid taking on the traditionally specialized role of "expert." See Einar Thorsud, "Democratization of Work and the Process of Organizational Change," *International Journal of Sociology* (Spring 1976), pp. 76–104. Our real hopes lie with institutional nonacademic people, although this is said for purposes of inclusion of everyone rather than exclusion of anyone.

Epilogue

1. P. A. Allum, *Italy—Republic without Government?* (New York: W. W. Norton and Co., 1973).
2. For documentation of the comparatively low political involvement of Italians and Czechs compared with North Americans and especially Yugoslavs, see Simona Ganassi Agger, *Urban Self-Management* (White Plains, N.Y.: M. E. Sharpe, English translation, 1978), chap. I; and to appreciate how low that involvement is compared with that of citizens of such other countries as Mexico, Germany, the United Kingdom, and the United States, see Gabriel A. Almond and Sidney Verba, *The Civic Culture* (Boston: Little, Brown and Co., 1963).
3. Walter Dean Burnham, "The End of American Party Politics," *Trans-action*, vol. 7 (December 1969), pp. 12–22, reprinted in Joseph R. Fiszman and Gene S. Poschman (eds.), *The American Political Arena*, 3rd ed. (Boston: Little, Brown and Co., 1972), p. 259.

Index

Langer, Susanne, 84
Language, 33, 60, 108, 131–133
    defined, 54
Lasswell, Harold O., 54, 110, 123
Laws, 90
Lay jury system, 136
Lefebvre, Henri, 96–99
Lenin, Vladimir Ilytch, 69, 175
Leninists, 174
Liberals, 2, 78, 122
Liberal welfare state, 122, 123
Literature, 51, 80
Living theater, 153
Love, 19–21

Marcuse, Herbert, 57, 74, 149–155,
    160, 161
Market values, 41
Marx, Karl, xii, 5–8, 14, 21, 22, 33, 34,
    37–38, 41, 50, 56, 78, 87, 98, 111,
    123, 144, 148–150
    on art, 51
    concept of production, 43
    double consciousness of, 59–71
    model of human beings, 3–6
Marxism, 122, 130
Marxists, 8, 33, 38, 70, 111, 149, 150,
    160, 174
Massachusetts Institute of Technology
    (MIT), 161
Maturity, 13, 110
    defined, 58–59
Medical and health care, 92–93
Mezzogiorno, 168
Mitchell, John, 166
Mobility in America, 116
Modern society, 13, 25
    developments of, 1
Monetary values, 42
Money, 14, 15, 35, 42, 43
Moro, Aldo, 167, 171, 173–175
Motivation, economic model of, 35
Multiple-party systems, 70
Mumford, Lewis, 65
Music, 29–33, 34, 51

Nagel, Ernest, 101–102, 104
Natanson, Maurice, 104–105, 107
Natural-social functionalism, 9–10
Nazis, 173
Needs (see Human needs)
New Critics in literature, 51
New Left, 149
New Philosophers (France), 123
New York City, 176
Nixon, Richard, 166
Noncommunist world, 70
Non-Marxists, 8

Objectification, 60
Ontological problem, 8
Open University (Britain), 134

Partialization of individuals, 16, 48
Partialized-person models, 48
Person-institution model, 27–29
Phenomenological approach, 105–107,
    137
    to art and aesthetics, 87
Philosophy, 7, 104, 105
Physics, 108
Police, 73, 76–78, 166
Politics and institutions, 56
Practice, defined, 54
Primal human moment, 12
Primary needs of human beings, 2–3,
    4, 8
    (See also Human needs)
Production, 6, 7, 36–38, 143–147
    Lefebvre on, 98–99
    Marx on, 43, 67
Productive force, 67
Productive labor, 7
Project SEED, 134
Pseudoproblems, x
Psychiatrists, 127
Psychosurgery, 112
Public Choice Society, 123

192

Red Brigades, 165, 171, 172, 174, 175, 177
Reification, 99
Religion, 8, 104
　　Marxist view, 43
Revolution, 67
　　in the sixties, 73–75
　　(*See also* Counterculture)
Rubin, Jerry, 74
Russian Revolution, 173

Sartre, Jean-Paul, 104
Schutz, Alfred, 104
Science, 8, 65
　　as institution, 101–105
Scientific method, 101, 108
Scientists, 27, 102–104, 108
Scandinavians, 46
Service professions, 93–94
Service society, 92
Sheets, Maxine, 84, 106
Sixties, 72–75, 132, 166, 169, 173
Skinner, B. F., 106
Smith, Adam, 6, 7, 33, 34, 62
Social psychology, 114
Socialists, 2, 6
Soviet Union, 4, 70, 123, 155, 159, 174
Specialization, 2, 142
Stalin, Joseph, 69, 159, 174
Students in the sixties, 73
Subinstitution, 40
Superstructural institutions, 8
Systems analysis, 10, 124–125
Systems Dynamics Group (MIT), 161
Systems scientists, 124–125

Talents, 28, 29, 46
Tautological labeling, 9
Terrorism, 166
Terrorists, 167, 171, 173, 175, 176
Third Reich, 174
Third World, 175
Time, 21–22

Toronto, Canada, 135
Total person, 16–18, 24, 54, 64, 75, 76, 81, 95, 98, 109, 113, 116, 125, 126, 128, 148, 158
　　models of, 40, 48
True consciousness, 55, 59, 71, 80, 81, 94, 112, 119, 161

Unemployment, 127, 128
　　in Italy, 168, 169
Unions, 58
United States, 70, 73, 78, 120, 134, 149, 166, 168, 173, 175
Universities in the sixties, 73
Urban guerrillas, 165, 173
Use values, 41, 154
Utilities, 41

Value of houses, 41, 42
Value-maximizing model of man, 21
Values (*see* Human values)
Van der Rohe, Mies, 81
Vickers, Geoffrey, 120–122
Vietnam War, 73–75

Watergate, 166, 173
Wealth, 7, 40
　　defined, 6
Wealth of Nations (Smith), 6
Weather Underground, 166
Weber, Max, 111
Weimar Republic, 167, 168
Welfare, 41
Welfare services, 92
Williams, Raymond, 51–53, 80, 130, 131
Women in Italy, 169
Work–leisure time dualism, 144
World Bank, 124
World War II, 134, 166

Yugoslavia, 70, 132, 155–158

193